Library of Congress Cataloging-in-Publication Data

Dr. Jessica Houston
Women's Secrets

ISBN 978-0-615-95183-6

Printed in the United States of America

BOOK DESIGNED BY
PENCILWORX DESIGN GROUP
WWW.PENCILWORX.COM

WOMEN'S SECRETS

IT'S TIME TO STOP SUFFERING IN SILENCE

Written By: Dr. Jessica Houston

TAKE
THE
FIRST
STEP
DOWN
A
NEW
ROAD

ABOUT THE AUTHOR

Dr. Jessica Houston, Ph.D., LMSW, has more than a decade of social work, counseling and higher education teaching experience. Throughout her career and personal life she has helped hundreds of individuals identify and fulfill their personal, educational and career goals. Her professional experience and educational achievements have earned her a remarkable reputation as an expert on vital matters like intimate partner violence, child sexual abuse, depression and low self-esteem.

WHAT ARE PEOPLE SAYING ABOUT DR. HOUSTON

Years ago I witnessed a light of care, concern, and compassion in a beautiful and brilliant young lady. The path that she has chosen and this effort to share what she has learned along the way is worth the time to read. Blessings are ahead be assured, when you read her book.

Dr. Nicholas Cooper-Lewter, LCSW
Sports Psychology Expert, Life Coach
CEO, Cooper Lewter Consulting, LLC

TABLE OF CONTENTS

:::::::::::::::::::::::::::::::

FOREWORD

:::::::::::::::::::::::::::::::::

Foreword by Dr. M. Dianna Hollins

It is with great pleasure and honor to be a part of a dynamic testimony and to read a self-evaluating literature piece of Dr. Jessica Houston. This captivating book permeates the truth and challenges of a woman. She provides the tools and strategies to overcome and pursue those areas of one's life that have been created to stagnate growth. This intriguing book has been birthed to elevate a person into his/her purpose. The reflection and sculpture of a successful woman is pronounced throughout each chapter of this book.

Dr. Houston allows the reader to share in her personal experiences and professional encounters. She also challenges the reader to regain and rejuvenate him/herself regardless of the pain and disappointments of life. As you read this book, you will be able to answer those questions that have been avoided and rejected by others. Therefore, it is of significant importance that the reader receives this book with the heart of change and a determined ear in order to go to his/her next level.

Dr. Hollins is a spiritual mentor,

pastor and author of the following books:

P.A.I.N. (Powerful Anointed in Neutral)

Volume 1: The Beginning

P.A.I.N. (Powerful Anointed in Neutral)

Volume 2: A Trimester Experience With No Gender

Pregnant With Purpose

40-Day Declaration of Power

DEDICATION

I would like to first and foremost, dedicate this book to my beautiful daughter Camille Houston. Camille, I am so grateful to have you in my life. Before you transformed my life I was existing, but I was not living. After making an amazing transformation, I can truly say that I am living my best life right now! Camille, you are my inspiration and the sun that brightens my day. I love you with all of my heart and soul. I would also like to dedicate this book to my amazing sister Jasmine Saxon. Thank you for believing in me and supporting me. Finally, this book is dedicated to my mother. Mom you are my best friend and my biggest cheerleader. Thank you for always being in my corner.

INTRODUCTION

Are you keeping any secrets? Are you suppressing any experiences? This book was written to help women understand the importance of addressing and moving beyond painful secrets and experiences. As a woman who has suppressed a tremendous amount of pain, I had to step back and identify the true source of my pain and unhappiness. Keeping secrets and suppressing past experiences may help you tune out painful experiences. However, suppression does not address the issue at its core. Therefore, suppression can only serve as a temporary coping mechanism.

In order to receive true healing, you must come face-to-face with your painful experiences. I have found that pain is a commonality among all of us. However, it is a phenomenon that most of us fear or are ultimately unwilling to discuss. Consequently, we have experiences that we try to suppress or forget because we believe that they are too painful to remember. However, at some point in our lives we must be transparent if we truly want to help someone else. Although I share my personal story throughout this book, this book is not about me at all. It is about making a decision to identify and address the issues that are impacting millions of women like you and me on a daily basis. Women are very nurturing individuals. However, in the midst of nurturing everyone else, we often forget to support and nurture ourselves. Women's Secrets will delve into many topics and issues that deserve to be discussed more often, such as dating and intimate partner violence, self-confidence and the importance of self-care. I will also share numerous strategies that will help transform you into the woman that you are destined to be. After reading this book, you will recognize the importance of being honest about your struggles and asking for help when you need it. You will also recognize the importance of seeking your purpose and pursuing your passion. Instead of focusing on your shortcomings, you will be inspired to focus on your strengths and available resources.

It was not easy for me to share my struggles and experiences throughout this book. However, I now understand that my experiences were not in vain. I am excited to know that I can use them to show women of various ages that change is possible. When you reach a certain level personally and/or professionally, it appears to the outside world that you have it all together. In fact, we can all make our lives appear to be perfect. We can all pretend to be happy, confident, and content with our lives. However, it is important that we are honest with ourselves and begin working towards making our desires a reality. Transforming the way that you view challenges and obstacles will help you accomplish much more than you have been able to accomplish in the past. Likewise, deciding to confront the very roadblocks that have been holding you back, will give you the confidence to move forward and expect victory in every aspect of your life. If you desire a husband and children, understand that you are whole and you are valuable right now. The biggest mistake you can ever make is to decide that you will only be happy once you reach a particular goal or milestone in life. Many times we sacrifice our happiness for what we believe will ultimately make us happier. Hence you commit to being unhappy over a period of weeks, months or even years. When you decide to delay your happiness, you miss out on many of the gifts and blessings that life has to offer because you are too focused on what you are lacking. It is important to understand that even when you reach your goal or milestone, there will be opportunities as well as challenges. For example, a woman without a husband or without children might envy a married woman with children and assume she has the perfect life. She is only focusing on the fact that this woman has a lifestyle that she would like to have one day. Unfortunately, she has no idea what types of challenges the woman she envies might be facing. Moreover, she probably does not know what it took for the married woman with children to be where she is today. The same scenario can be applied to the professional woman with multiple degrees who appears to be quickly climbing the corporate ladder. First, we have to understand that success does not come without sacrifice. Therefore, when you have a goal or a strong desire to move to the next level, you must be disciplined and prepared to sacrifice something. The sacrifice may be financial, loss of friends, loss of time, loss of sleep and so forth.

For this reason, you should keep in mind that things are not always what they seem. Even the woman who appears to have it all together has past and current struggles. Problems are inevitable. However, it is how we respond to problems that separate those who are happy from those who are unhappy. My plan is to educate, encourage and empower women to have an open and honest discussion about topics and issues that can be painful. My goal is also to provide women with the tools that they need to be happy with themselves and excited about their future. I know that there are many women who have talents that are not being utilized, simply because they do not have confidence in themselves and their abilities. I truly believe that you can reach your full potential if you step out of your comfort zone and begin to identify and address the issues and fears that have been holding you back over the years. I have poured my heart and spirit into this book and I am confident that it will be a blessing to you, your family and your friends. The benefits of this book go far beyond you as an individual. The benefits extend, because a happier and more confident you means that you will be a better mom, wife, sister, aunt, girlfriend and friend. It also means that you will see an increase in your overall level of life satisfaction. If you are willing to implement the strategies identified in this book, you will be able to make a radical transformation. Thank you in advance for allowing this book to serve as your guide as you continue to grow and reach new levels.

How I Came to See Myself

*Self-perception significantly impacts
many areas of our lives.*

*Having a positive view of ourselves can
give us the confidence that we
need to accept challenges
and reach our full potential.*

Self-perception significantly impacts many areas of our lives. Having a positive view of ourselves can give us the confidence that we need to accept challenges and reach our full potential. On the other hand, having a negative view of ourselves can hinder our ability to reach our full potential. Although low self-esteem is often discussed in relation to body dissatisfaction, it is important to note that someone can have low self-esteem related to their mental and physical abilities as well. When you have low self-confidence or low self-esteem you are more likely to have a negative view of yourself and your capabilities. Low self-esteem can prevent highly talented individuals from reaching their full potential. In fact, it can be the sole factor that prevents people from speaking up for themselves, going to college, pursuing a career, or leaving an abusive relationship. In essence, low self-esteem can keep you in a holding pattern, if it is never confronted. In addition to being a barrier to success, low self-esteem also hinders life satisfaction. Low self-esteem has been linked to eating disorders, depression, and anxiety. It has also been linked to being involved in dysfunctional relationships, being promiscuous, lacking assertiveness, and living with a constant fear of rejection.

A well-known psychologist by the name of Albert Bandura actually conducted an extensive amount of research related to self-esteem, and as a result, developed the self-efficacy theory. Self-Efficacy involves believing in your capabilities to perform well, even in the midst of a challenge. The self-efficacy theory affirms that how you view yourself contributes to how you function in four major areas of your life. The four areas are:

cognitive, motivational, emotional, and choice. Once we realize that our self-esteem impacts our cognitive abilities, our level of motivation, our emotional state, and the choices we make, we can then truly conceptualize how important it is to have a positive view of ourselves and our abilities. When we have confidence in ourselves and our abilities, our level of functioning is increased. Self-efficacy is a great attribute to have, because it encourages higher expectations and positive dispositions. Albert Bandura suggests that people who have a high perceived self-efficacy, approach difficult tasks as challenges to be mastered rather than threats to be avoided. This theory is powerful, because it helps us recognize the importance of having a positive self-concept. Having a negative view of ourselves severely limits our ability to utilize our skills, gifts, and talents. Perhaps this explains why so many people never reach their full potential.

My Story

Self-esteem, self-value, and self-worth are topics that are important for women and girls to discuss. Women are often portrayed and discussed in derogatory ways in rap lyrics, music videos, and magazines. Moreover, beauty is often defined by the women who grace the covers of major magazines. Subsequently, we have teens and adolescents with symptoms of low-self esteem. These same teens and adolescents also have a very poor understanding about their value and self-worth. Nevertheless, these topics are not being discussed on a consistent basis. For years I struggled with low self-esteem. I would look in the mirror and become deeply frustrated. I would then look at every part of my body and find something wrong with it. On the outside, I appeared to be very self-confident. However, on the inside I was beyond disappointed about the way I looked. As a pre-teen, I wished that my skin was lighter. I also wished that my nose was smaller, and hoped that my breasts would grow larger. I envied the girls who had a lighter complexion and seemed to have the physical appearance that I dreamed about. As I grew older, it was difficult to accept that my skin tone, my nose, and my breasts were here to stay.

I have always received compliments about my physical appearance. People would say "you are so pretty." Guys would tell me that I was "fine." Teachers would tell me that I was "smart." But, those words never mattered to me. Only my opinion mattered, and I did not like my appearance. Yes, I earned excellent grades, but I did not believe that I was smart. It's amazing how low self-esteem can interfere with multiple areas of our lives. For some reason, I kept a mediocre attitude about every aspect of my life. If someone asked me what my strengths were, it initially took me a while to identify them. However, I eventually became skilled enough to memorize a response that made the individual asking the question believe that I had it all together. Unfortunately, while I knew what to say, I did not actually believe the responses that I gave to others.

As I transitioned to college, the stakes were much higher. There were thousands of attractive girls on campus. So, in order to compete, I would wear revealing clothing. I wore the short shorts, halter tops, miniskirts, extra tight jeans, and I would not be caught anywhere without high heels. When I dressed provocatively, I received an enormous amount of attention from men and this made me feel better. I looked forward to stepping out and having guys stop in their tracks to talk to me and ask me for my number. However, the excitement and satisfaction was only temporary. Because, once I was alone, and in front of the mirror, I would immediately go back to the same frame of mind. There was always an internal conflict about how I saw myself. It did not matter how good my life was or appeared to be, I was unhappy. Although it looked like I had it all together, I was never my best self.

It was not until my mid 20's that I finally began to become somewhat comfortable in my own skin. I was finally able to look in the mirror and not wish that my skin was lighter. However, I still disliked my nose, my breasts, my legs, my knees, my hips, and my stomach. I would frequently watch music videos, and those women did not appear to have any of the flaws that I had. I was unhappy with myself, but not a single person knew it but me. It was to the point where even when I was dating, I would secretly wonder why my boyfriend was interested in me. I would think, "doesn't he see this huge nose?" This negative body image had consumed me to the extent that I would accept behavior from people that I should not have accepted. Unfortunately, I accepted a great deal of mistreatment, because I believed that my looks would hinder me from finding another boyfriend.

This brings me to a question that I have for you, "do you truly recognize your value?" Sometimes others recognize our value more than we do. Unfortunately, when this happens they offer us less and we accept it without thinking twice. It took me a long time to recognize my value. It never crossed my mind that I had qualities, skills, and attributes that made me unique and valuable. In fact, before recognizing my value, it never crossed my mind that I deserved the best in my personal as well as my professional life. Once I recognized my value, I began expecting more and in return, I began receiving more. People who do not recognize their value are typically unsatisfied with their lives. Some of the consequences of not recognizing your value includes but is not limited to poor treatment, lower wages, and overall mediocre living. In essence, when you do not believe that you are worth more, you are willing to accept much less than you deserve.

I wasted far too many years of my life drowning in self pity. The worst part of that scenario is that I can never get those years back. You should not waste another moment wishing that you could have the relationship, financial stability, or career that you desire. Your opportunities are limitless. However, you must understand what you have to offer and believe that you deserve the best. Moreover, you must recognize your potential and never settle for mediocrity. When you realize that you deserve more, you will begin to expect more. Knowing your value creates an opportunity for you to set high expectations. I challenge you to list at least three strengths that make you valuable. Keep these three items at the forefront of your mind and continually remind yourself that you will no longer accept poor or even mediocre treatment. You deserve the best and you should not expect or accept anything less than the best.

I will share more about the abusive relationship that I was involved in from age 17-22 in a later chapter. However, I believe that it is fitting to mention it here, because my low self-esteem is the reason why I stayed in a relationship with him for so long. In addition to being physically abused, he cheated on me multiple times, and even had a second child with the mother of his first child, while we were supposed to be in a monogamous relationship. I wanted to leave, but I was not strong enough. He was popular, he was on the basketball team, he was the star of the football team, and I was known as HIS girlfriend. In my eyes, I was lucky that he loved me as much as he did. The girls on campus wanted him, but he wanted me, and for me that was enough.

Unfortunately, I took this same mind-set into my marriage. I initially accepted mediocre and sometimes poor treatment. I also continued to deal with low self-confidence and it caused a lot of unnecessary conflicts. My husband wondered why I was not quite interested in dressing sexy. He would tell me that he liked my body and I honestly could not understand why. It was amazing how I shifted from always wearing revealing clothing, to being extremely conservative. Despite what my husband would tell me, I just could not get past the way I felt about myself. I would exercise, get my hair done, get a pedicure, go shopping.....but in the end, I still felt the same way. I felt the same way, because I continued to suppress my feelings and avoided working through my issues. It is imperative that you work on your inner being, before attempting to perform a makeover on your outer being. It is moot to present as beautiful and confident on the outside, while feeling hopeless and empty on the inside. At some point we must stop running from our struggles and our fears. Pushing through your fears and tackling your struggles will allow you to finally reach a place of victory and life satisfaction.

It was not until I gave birth to my daughter in February 2012, that I started the process of accepting me for who I am. As a mother, I do not want my daughter to settle for less. I want her to know that she is beautiful and capable of exceeding all of her personal and professional goals. It took a while, but now I realize that many of the women portrayed on television are just as imperfect as I am. The only difference is that, they can and will pay for a personal trainer, a chef, a nanny, a surgeon, and so forth. The women portrayed on television and in the magazines have an entire team of people who help them become the person that we see in the spotlight. It never occurred to me that scars and other perceived imperfections are often removed before the photos are released to the public. Have I actually arrived to the place where I can look in the mirror and say "I Love Me?" Yes, I have. However, I am still a work in progress. Admitting all of these personal thoughts, experiences, and feelings are extremely difficult. However, I know that there are other women out there feeling the same way and they need to know that they are not alone. The good news is that I have taken the first step required for healing to begin. As long as I suppress my feelings,

I cannot help myself and I cannot help others. Life is too short for me to waste another minute having a pity party over my physical appearance. If I do not love myself or have confidence in myself, then who will? At this point in my life, I am going to "work" what I have, and so should you!

Moving Forward

Knowing the risks associated with low self-esteem, it is critical that we address this issue. It is time to acknowledge that low self-esteem, low self-confidence, and feelings of low self-worth are far too prevalent among young girls and women. Many research studies have found that the media plays a pivotal role in our perception of what is beautiful and what is not. Today, we see half clothed women in magazines, movies, commercials, and so forth. Unfortunately, we have allowed the media to define beauty. Although we know that the images portrayed in the media can distort how a young girl views herself, these images sell, and therefore are here to stay. There are several ways that we can begin to revitalize our thinking and improve our view of ourselves and our abilities. First, we need to be honest about our feelings. Once we are honest about our feelings, we can begin the process of healing. Second, we need to practice positive thinking on a daily basis. Third, we need to discover our purpose, and finally, we need to help and encourage others.

It's easy to fool everyone else into thinking that we are confident in ourselves and our abilities. It's easy to say 'I love myself and I love the way I look." However, the hard part is coming to terms with how you truly view yourself and your abilities. Is it possible that low self-confidence is holding you back from pursuing your goals and your dreams? Is possible that low-self confidence is keeping you in a relationship that you know is not in your best interest? Sorensen (2006) compares low self-esteem to wearing a mask. She suggests that individuals with low self-esteem try to look like they are confident when they feel inadequate and try to behave as though everything is okay, when that is not how they feel at all. For example, in college as well as in the professional workforce, most people believed that I had a high level of self-confidence. However, it was actually a façade, to mask self-loathing. When you accept the challenge of being honest about your feelings, you will begin to feel a huge weight being lifted off of your shoulders. It is difficult to fully heal, as long as your pain is masked and remains hidden.

In order to transition from self-doubt to self-confidence, you must be willing to change your way of thinking. Practicing positive thinking is an important challenge to accomplish as you begin to change the way that you view yourself and your capabilities. Positive thinking is not just a catchy phrase. It has worked for me and it can work for you as well. However, you must make a conscious decision to view your challenges from a different perspective. Perhaps you can view your challenges as an opportunity to grow. Positive thinking has two primary benefits. First, it encourages you to transform your normal way of thinking. The mind has a great deal of control over your behavior. Therefore, in every circumstance or situation, you have a choice. You can either think positively or negatively.

We are often tempted to take a negative perspective, but we should always strive to think positively. This might mean that you perceive a setback as temporary rather than permanent. Therefore, instead of becoming depressed, you would begin developing a new and better plan. When we adopt positive thinking, it increases our chances of actually seeing a positive outcome. Focusing on our strengths and positive attributes can have a positive impact on our emotional and physical well-being. At some point we all encounter various issues and struggles. However, positive thinking can replace thoughts of despair and hopelessness that might be present during difficult times. Secondly, positive thinking can be utilized in any setting or situation. For example, it can be applied at work, at school, at home, or in any tough situation. It can be argued that negative views of self and negative thinking do not impact outcome. However, research supports the notion that our beliefs contribute significantly to the choices we make, the effort we expend, how long we persevere in the face of a challenge, and the degree of anxiety or confidence that we bring to various challenges and tasks (Swann, Chang-Schneider, & McClarty, 2007). The choice is yours, but I truly hope that you will begin to incorporate positive thinking into every aspect of your life.

When we enter elementary school, we are often asked: what do you want to be when you grow up? I can recall being asked this question time after time and I can remember changing my answer from teacher, to lawyer, to judge, to pediatrician, and then back to teacher again. Even when I went to college,

I had an idea of what I wanted to do, but I was not quite sure. When I finally decided that social work was my profession of choice, the next question was: why would you choose to be a social worker? Many people had formulated an opinion about the social work profession and dwelled on the fact that social workers did not make much money. While everyone meant well, what they really should have encouraged me to do is find my passion and discover my purpose. I cannot emphasize enough, how important it is to discover your purpose for being here on this earth. Everyone was placed here for a reason and when you find that reason, you are going to have a new perspective on life.

I have gone through periods when I was so depressed that it did not matter to me if I lived or not.

During those times, I had no idea why I was here. I had low self-confidence, I was involved in a physically and emotionally abusive relationship, and I believed that I did not have any value. I knew that I loved to help others, but that was it. While I was able to point out the strengths and abilities of others, I could not seem to identify my own. While I could encourage others, I could not encourage myself. Finally, I began reading more, praying more, and reflecting upon what it was that truly made me happy. Once I slowed down, de-cluttered my mind, and sought clarity, I was able to discover why I was placed on this earth. Discovering your purpose is a deliberate process. It is not an overnight process and it is not something that is automatic. You must clear out all of your distractions, even the ones that you enjoy! You must also take the time to think about what comes to you easily, what your interests are, and what brings you joy. I can vividly remember the day that I discovered my purpose. I woke up at 4am and I wrote down my thoughts at that very moment. It was an experience that I cannot fully describe with words. The moment the light bulb went off, I began reflecting on my life and thanking God for covering me and protecting me, when I behaved irrationally during my 20's. I thought about the many risks that I took and how he still allowed me to be blessed with a family, a home, a car, and several educational and professional accomplishments. Your experience will likely be different from my experience. However, I guarantee that when you discover your purpose, your life will change for the better.

Helping and encouraging others is the final piece to this puzzle. It is extremely important that we move towards developing a positive view of ourselves and our capabilities. Right now you might be wondering how helping and encouraging someone else could possibly benefit you. First, helping someone else can be very therapeutic. Second, now that you understand the importance of having a positive self-concept, you should want to share what you now know with others. Finally, think about how you can give someone a second chance at life, just by sharing your story and letting them know that they are capable of living a joy filled and victorious life. Most times, our feelings and beliefs about ourselves or our situation are over-exaggerated. For this reason, we often think ourselves into a state of depression. If you have a resource that you can share or just a few encouraging words, please do not hold back. Everyone deserves to believe in themselves. Everyone deserves to love themselves, and everyone deserves to accept nothing less than the best. While in church one Sunday, my pastor said, "no one has everything, but everyone has something." Those words have resonated with me and I hope that they resonate with you as well. As you continue to grow, remember to be honest about your feelings, practice positive thinking, discover your purpose, and strive to help and encourage others. Remember that growth is a continuous process. The moment that you believe that there is nothing more for you to learn, is the moment that you stop growing.

My next steps to get to the next level

_____

_____

_____

_____

_____

_____

_____

_____

_____

_____

_____

The Poverty Experience

Poverty impacts millions

of children every year.

It can affect anyone at any time

and it is not confined to

one particular race or culture.

Poverty impacts millions of children every year. It can affect anyone at any time and it is not confined to one particular race or culture. Poverty may be long-term (generational) or short-term (situational). Poverty can bring along a great deal of pain, insecurity and feelings of inferiority. When someone lives in poverty that person does not have the money or resources needed to meet what society deems basic needs. Basic needs include but are not limited to food, shelter, clothing, running water and electricity. I can speak candidly about poverty, because as a child, I experienced poverty. There are certainly different levels of poverty and some individuals have experienced what I call extreme poverty.

Although I did not experience extreme poverty, I did experience generational poverty. I did not truly understand the extent of our financial struggles until I was about 14 years-old. As a child, I can remember going with my mother to the Department of Children and Family Services (DFCS). We would be there for hours, waiting for her to speak with a case manager. I can also remember her having to answer a series of personal questions that made her feel uncomfortable. Our need for government assistance never made me feel as though we were poor because most of the people we associated with were receiving government assistance as well. It actually took me a while to realize that my experience was different from those who grew up in a middle-class family. As a family, we had a great deal of financial difficulties but I guess it just did not occur to me that we were poor. Today, celebrities continue to boast about their cars, houses, money and their lifestyles. For this reason, it is likely that children today are more aware of their family's financial status.

My Story

My mother gave birth to me when she was 19 years-old. Although, she was an adult, she did not have the income or resources necessary to adequately provide for herself and a baby. She was the oldest of six children and she was the only one, out of six siblings, to earn a high school diploma. After completing high school, my biological father went to college and went on to earn a law degree. My paternal grandparents offered to take care of me if my mother chose to go off to college, but she declined the offer because she did not want to place the responsibility of caring for me on someone else. At one point my mother enrolled in an associate degree program at a community college. However, she did not complete the program. She has always been a strong woman and she was always willing to do what she needed to do to take care of me. She began dating my stepfather when I was an infant. Our family eventually grew from a family of four to a family of six. Although my mother told me that he was not my biological father, I have always called my stepfather, dad. Therefore, I will refer to him as dad from this point forward.

Despite my dad's strong work ethic, it was difficult for my family to make ends meet. Between working two jobs and frequenting nightclubs, he was often away from home. In retrospect, we probably would have been in a better position financially if our finances were appropriately managed. For example, my dad would often splurge to maintain a certain image. As a result, someone on the outside looking in probably assumed we were financially stable. However, this was not the case. For example, we were able to move from a two-bedroom apartment in Pompano Beach, Florida, to a two-bedroom house in Fort Lauderdale,

Florida. However, we could not afford the maintenance on our house. Consequently, we had a home that needed a great deal of work done. I can remember having to put pots in several areas of our house every time it rained. We literally had holes in our ceiling. I can even remember seeing mushrooms inside, which I now believe came from the moisture build up inside of our house. After several years of living in a home that we could not maintain and could not afford, we lost our home to fore-closure and had to move out. From there we lived with my dad's mom until we could find another apartment. We moved into another two-bedroom apartment and eventually had to move again. The cycle of moving and living with relatives for short periods of time, continued un-til I was 14. When I was 15, we were able to transition into public housing and this allowed us to remain at one residence for several years. Some of you might be wondering how I could possibly live in poverty when I had a biological father who was an attorney. Unfortunately, my mother decided not to place my biological father on formal child support and he opted to provide the bare minimum. Therefore, she only collected a small amount of money from him every month. I truly believe that my biological father loved me but I never understood why I had to struggle when I had a father who was a successful attorney.

I always thought that a homeless individual was someone who was sleeping on the streets or sleeping in their car. However, after entering the field of social work, I realized that an individual is considered home-less if he or she does not have an adequate and consistent residence due to lack of financial resources. This revelation was an eye-opener because I never would have identified myself as homeless. Although we struggled financially and moved several times, I consistently performed well in school. At this point in my life, I am very grateful that my mother always reinforced the importance of education. Despite what may have been going on in our lives at the time, she made sure that I attended school every day.

Next, I can vividly remember dreading going into a store with food stamps. Now, there are EBT cards, but during that time period we had a book of food stamps. The look of the stamps made it quite obvious that we were paying with food stamps instead of cash. I was just as embarrassed when we would go into consignment shops to purchase second hand clothing, shoes, furniture, etc. I would always say: Mom, I do not want to go in there because one of my friends might see me, can I stay in the car? Her reply was always, "well if they see you in there that means that they were in there too." I must say that she was right because whenever I did see a classmate in the consignment shop, they always seemed just as embarrassed as I was.

My experiences with poverty, helped mold me into the woman that I am today. Perhaps if I did not know what it felt like to live in public or substandard housing, I would not have had the drive to go to college and break the cycle of generational poverty. Perhaps if I did not know what it felt like to be on the receiving end of social services, I would not have had the desire to major in social work. Looking back, I am amazed at what my parents were able to accomplish with very little resources. Knowing what it is like to be in need makes me very excited about being a part of the "helping profession." I find the field of social work to be extremely rewarding because now I have an opportunity to give back and I am enjoying every minute of it.

The Impact of Poverty

I found it important to dedicate a chapter of this book to poverty because the experience of poverty goes far beyond not having money and resources. Poverty plays a role in our decision making abilities, environment, what we value, how we communicate and the types of people we have in our circle. According to the US Census Bureau, in 2012, more than 46 million Americans were living in poverty. Much of the research related to poverty shows that children who grow up in poverty are more likely to drop out of school, live in substandard housing, be exposed to drugs and violence and experience higher levels of stress. As I will discuss later, children in poverty are also more likely to be victims of child abuse or neglect. All of these risk factors can lead to poor social, emotional and financial outcomes during adulthood. Hence, many of the negative and painful experiences that occurred as a result of poverty must be addressed. Similar to many of the other issues discussed in this book, poverty can be a barrier to happiness and success. For this reason, poverty is an issue that deserves attention.

Although many individuals have the belief that we all have the same educational opportunities, research has shown that there is a significant correlation between poverty and lower quality educational opportunities. One obvious difference between children in poverty and children in middle class families is the type of environment that they engage in on a daily basis. Teens in poverty often have a great deal of responsibility when they leave school. Some work part-time, while others are cooking dinner, cleaning the house and possibly caring for younger siblings. A teen with this much responsibility is likely to have difficulty keeping up with homework and time consuming projects.

Additionally, schools might request that students have tablets, binders and flash drives, amongst many other supplies. These requests might seem small to a middle class teacher. However, for a family who is already struggling, purchasing supplies can be a major financial setback. It is also important to think about teachers who request that a major project or assignment be typed. Even if the student has access to a computer, he or she might not have access to a printer. I am sharing these examples because such requirements along with the way that schools are structured can be barriers for poverty stricken children. Low-income families are trying to meet their basic needs and they are often under a significant amount of stress. Equally important, children in poverty are less likely to have access to tutoring, technology, high quality schools and positive adult role models.

Additionally, poverty-stricken families are involved with the Department of Family and Children Services at a much higher rate than other families. The reasons for being involved with DFCS may vary. However any involvement with DFCS can be stressful and the process typically involves an in-depth investigation to determine whether or not the allegations of abuse and or neglect are true. Allegations are deemed substantiated or true when parents are not meeting the basic needs of their children, have inappropriately disciplined their children or failed to provide adequate supervision. Families in poverty are also more likely to live in an unsafe environment, where many are exposed to or involved in domestic violence, alcoholism and drug use. For this reason, we often find that children living in poverty have high rates of absenteeism and dropping out of school. In fact, Almeida, Johnson, and Steinberg (2006) suggested that the primary factor associated with dropping out of school is a student's socioeconomic status. Socioeconomic inequalities in education have been widely investigated and researchers have found that socioeconomically disadvantaged children are less likely to experience school success. We must work together to ensure that children who are at high risk of dropping out of school due to limited resources receive the support needed to break the cycle of generational poverty.

As a result of living in poverty, I did not have the best communication skills. However, my love for reading, writing and attending school helped me expand my vocabulary and speak better than most of my friends. For instance, I remember speaking with a police officer about a report that was filed against a friend when I was 17 or 18 years of age. The officer seemed shocked by my ability to articulate what I had witnessed. He said, "young lady you are very articulate." This was the first time that I heard it phrased that way, what was normally said was "you talk white." I now recognize such commentary as one of many negative viewpoints held among children in poverty. I was articulate when I felt that I needed to be articulate. However, when I was with family and friends, I was not articulate at all. Unfortunately I assumed that I needed to speak one way at home and a different way in front of teachers or other individuals I considered to be important. As a result, I had to speak slower so that I could figure out what to say next. Even as an adult I struggle to remain articulate at home or in a relaxed environment. It's like a light switch that I can turn off and on as needed.

Finally, poverty had a direct impact on what I valued as a teen and as a young adult. I valued keeping up with trendy hairstyles. If you were to look at pictures from my teen years, you would be amused by the types of hairstyles that I managed to create. One week my hair would be blue and the next week it may have been purple or some other odd color. I also valued gold jewelry, real or fake, along with nice clothing and shoes. When I visited my biological father and his wife, I would hear comments about my hair and attire that were quite mean. Some of the terms used to describe me were thug, ghetto and so forth. These comments would not necessarily come from my father but individuals in his circle would make them. Fortunately, there was one person living a middle class lifestyle who never judged me and always showed me respect: my stepmother's mom. This woman was a true blessing and took me under her wing when I was only 10 years of age. She sent me meaningful cards and financial contributions when I completed high school, earned my bachelor's degree, master's degree, and even upon earning my doctoral degree. She even sent me a card with a $1,000 check to help pay for my wedding. Lastly, she sent a gift card for my baby shower and always purchases something for my daughter for Christmas and her birthday! She has no idea how much I appreciated her growing up. I knew that she believed in me and I wanted to make her proud. Today, she knows without a doubt that she is near and dear to my heart.

Yes, I was poor and what I liked differed from those who led different lifestyles. However, I could not help if I liked purple hair, purple contacts and big hoop earrings. This was who I was and such cultural aesthetics were a reflection of what I saw every day. Even when I transitioned to college, I still valued the same things. So, the hairstyles, colored contacts and hoop earrings continued. I also added tattoos to the mix and then I was really referred to as a thug. Reactions to my appearance would hurt me so badly that I had to talk to my mom about my feelings each time I returned from a visit with my biological father. She would always tell me not to worry about what they said or thought about me. She often said, "Jessica, trust me, you will prove them wrong one day." Needless to say, she was absolutely correct. Who would have thought that I would earn a Ph.D. and teach college level courses in my mid-thirties?

As a teen and young adult, I enjoyed learning but I really did not understand the true value of education, until I began working in the field of social work. When I was offered a job in Macon, Georgia, I was elated and extremely excited about the salary that was offered. I was only 23 years of age and I was offered a salary that allowed me to pay all of my bills. I was also able to help my mom purchase needed items for my siblings, contribute a little to my savings account and still have money left over. As you can see, I valued relationships and helping my family as well. My passion and desire to help others is a gift. Unfortunately, I have found that others will sometimes take advantage of my willingness to give. Eventually this led me to realize that I cannot resolve everyone else's issues and I can only give so much. There were times when I helped others so much that I neglected myself. This was something that I did unconsciously and it took my husband to point out that truth to me. Honestly, the first time that he brought this truth to my attention, I was very upset. However, once I moved beyond the anger, I had to admit that he was right.

Moving Beyond Poverty

I was considered an at-risk child because of the many issues that I endured as a child and as a teen. Although I encountered many teachers throughout my life, it was not until my senior year of college that a teacher took the time to really get to know me. This particular teacher encouraged me and told me I had the potential to earn a doctorate degree. This is notable because I should have come into contact with a positive adult who cared enough to get to know me well before I was a senior in college. His encouragement and positivity was important. For this reason, I never forgot him and have always kept in contact with him. To be honest, I thought my professor was out of his mind when he predicted that I would earn a doctorate degree and travel the world for speaking engagements. However, there was a small piece of me that believed him for some reason. He wrote a recommendation for me when I applied for graduate school. He even reviewed my essay to ensure that it was well-written. When someone takes the time to show you that they genuinely care about you, it truly makes a difference.

Although statistics suggest that I was at high risk of being a high school dropout, I still managed to graduate from high school and attend college. No one offered to help with my college application or financial aid application. However, I took the initiative to complete them on my own. In retrospect, it would have been great if I did have someone to assist me with the college application process. I believe that I was the exception, simply because I enjoyed learning and I had a family who valued education. Unfortunately, there are millions of adults out there who had the same potential I did, but they did not finish high school or attend college. Many of the adults who did not receive the guidance and support they needed during their youthful years are incarcerated, homeless, working minimum wage jobs and possibly depending on the federal government for financial support.

I believe that we have to change our perspective on poverty. We must stop promoting the stereotype that all individuals in poverty are lazy. It does not offer a solution and further ignites the idea that we should not help individuals and families experiencing poverty. Before passing judgment on someone, think about whether or not you have done anything to help someone in need. Just think about how many futures we can make brighter by simply helping one child or adult realize their potential. Do you have items like clothing, furniture and shoes that are merely taking up space in your home? Perhaps you should go through your closets and donate anything that you have not worn in the last year. Although I benefited greatly from second hand items, there were many times when I held on to items that I did not use. Now, I go through my closets at least twice per year and donate items that are taking up space, even if they are still new.

If you are a teen or young adult in the midst of financial difficulty, please do not give up. Your past and even your current experiences do not determine your destiny. The more opposition you face, the more effort you should expend on pursuing the lifestyle you desire. It can be tempting to quit school and get a low or mediocre paying job. However, when you drop out of school, you limit the number of opportunities you have to reach your financial goals. You also limit the possibilities of future generations. You can develop a generation that does not have to live paycheck to paycheck or barely make ends meet. I know that college is not for everyone. However, it is imperative that you learn a trade or skill that will help you stand out from everyone else. I understand that it can be difficult to delay gratification and have the discipline required to remain in school when others are working and appear to be doing well. However, in the long term, your hard work and dedication will pay off and you will have the career and the financial stability that will change your life for the better.

My next steps to get to the next level

_____

_____

_____

_____

_____

_____

_____

_____

_____

_____

_____

Money
Matters

We discuss money often as a society

yet we rarely have the discussions that

we need to have about money.

Money management is extremely

important and we must continually expand

our knowledge base in the area of finances.

We discuss money often as a society yet we rarely have the discussions that we need to have about money. Money management is extremely important and we must continually expand our knowledge base in the area of finances. There are households where women manage the finances, there are households where men manage the finances and there are households where finances are managed as a joint partnership. Nonetheless, even if one person is the primary money manager, both parties should be knowledgeable about the financial state of their household. The individual who is responsible for money management should be skilled enough to ensure that the budget is well balanced. For example, if you have a shopping or splurging habit, you probably should not be the money manager for your household. In order to meet your basic needs, pay your bills on time, obtain credit and feel adequately prepared for unexpected or future expenses, you must understand how to manage your finances properly.

The purpose of this chapter is to motivate you to improve the way you manage your money. When debt is high and money is low, it can be difficult to focus on other needs and desires. It is also difficult to truly be happy when your finances are not in order. Splurging on yourself or your family may provide short-term happiness. However, it ultimately leads to distress and anxiety, which can negatively impact your psychological, behavioral and physical health. Distress can also lead to anger, physical aggression, insomnia, hypertension and a host of other consequences. It is also good to keep in mind that mismanaging money can ruin friendships and family relationships. How many times have you had to borrow money from a friend or relative? How many times have you had to lend money to a friend or relative? I would like to mention that lending money can create tension when a relative or friend borrows money and does not pay it back. Unfortunately, this type of situation happens far too often and is responsible for ruining a host of relationships that started out great.

This chapter is significant because women must take care of their financial health, just as they would take care of their physical health. However, I realize that many women are not aware of their financial well being, their credit to debt ratio or their credit score. I also realize that there are women who are responsible for their household finances but they are consistently mismanaging their money. Poor money management is an issue that can be masked and suppressed but it is time for women to become financially healthy and make sound financial decisions. In order to accomplish this goal, women must be honest about their current situation and be willing to make and sustain changes in their spending and saving habits. I will share several strategies and principles that women can use to mitigate the consequences of poor money management. I will also share my personal story on some of the poor financial decisions that I have made in the past.

We live in a society where consumers purchase now and pay later. We are always receiving solicitation from credit card companies who count on us to spend more than we can afford to pay off at the end of each billing cycle. When you pay your credit card balance in full every month, you do not pay any interest on your purchases. Therefore, the credit card company does not make a profit. However, if you are late making a payment or if you carry a balance on your credit card, you are contributing to the profits earned by credit card companies. It is unfortunate that credit is often extended to individuals who cannot afford to pay for the credit that they have been offered through banks or other lenders. Subsequently, those who accept the offer are likely to make purchases that max out their credit card and ultimately ruin their credit. For example, as an 18 year old college student without any income, I was offered multiple credit cards and I accepted all of them. I can remember going to the mall with friends and being offered store credit on the spot. We had no idea what a credit score was and we certainly did not understand that the money spent would need to be paid back at some point. In our minds, credit cards gave us access to clothing, shoes and any other item we wanted to purchase. For years, I paid the minimum balance due, while my balance grew larger and larger. The interest rates on all of my credit cards were extremely high and eventually reached a point where I was not even able to afford the minimum balance due. I became frustrated and every month the interest and fees continued to add up. As a result of spending money that I did not have, I accumulated more than $10,000 in credit card debt. I eventually decided to close all of my credit cards because the interest and late payment fees were adding up quickly. Once I accepted my first job as a social worker, I was ready to face the disaster I created. Fortunately, with the assistance of my biological father, I was able to settle with all of the collection agencies for a lower pay-off amount.

As adults we must accept responsibility for our behaviors and not spend more money than we earn. It may temporarily feel good to have nice clothing, electronics and other material items you can't truly afford. However, when you continue to live beyond your means, you will eventually find yourself in a financial crisis. Terms such as credit,

debt and net worth are used casually. It is great to know these financial terms. However, it is more important that you truly understand
the ramifications of opening multiple lines of credit, accumulating too
much debt and improperly managing finances. So, for starters, what
are your beliefs about money? Do you believe that money equates to
status? Do you believe money equates to security? Should individuals live above their earned income, within their earned income, or be-
neath their earned income? Do you know how much money comes
into your home on a monthly basis and how much goes out? Do you
know your credit score? Do you pull your credit report at least once per
year? These are the types of questions that must be asked to determine
whether or not you are in a position to create wealth.

Money management may not be a topic of interest to you but it is a
topic that must be discussed. Especially, if you struggle in the area of
money management. It is important to note that avoiding an issue does
not resolve it and if you continue to avoid the elephant in the room,
your financial situation will never improve. Equally important, we should
never live as though we earn more money than we actually bring home.
In fact, individuals who choose to do so are heading towards a path of
destruction. Money management should matter to you whether you
are single, dating or married. If you have children, the topic of money
should be extremely important to you because you should strive to create generational wealth. Meaning, you should strive to create wealth
that does not end with your generation. Moreover, you should want to
model appropriate money management skills for your children. Growing up in poverty, I really did not know much about money management. However, through the process of trial and error along with edu-

cating myself in this area, I have learned how to appropriately manage my finances. I can vividly remember two important principles taught by my undergraduate economics professor. The first principle was, "always pay your-self first." Paying yourself first involves contributing to your savings account. However, it does not refer to purchasing an expensive gift for yourself. The second principle was, "spend some, save some and give some." In other words, do not place all of your money into one category. You are allowed to treat yourself but you should also develop a habit of saving. Finally, you should give if you can afford to do so. I challenge you to become serious about your finances and to save for your future, if you are not saving already. Finally, I challenge you to examine your credit to debt ratio and your current spending habits.

Spending and Saving

How you spend and how you save are important aspects of the money management process. The first rule of spending is to avoid making large purchases on impulse. The excitement of taking advantage of a great deal on a car, television, dining set and so forth can push you to purchase a product on impulse. I have made large purchases on impulse and later found myself regretting it. Buyer's remorse is awful, especially when you cannot return the item. I suggest that you do research to see if you can find a better deal with another vendor. I also suggest that you give yourself at least a 24 hour period to decide whether or not you truly would like to purchase the item. There are times when stores and dealerships have a limited timeframe for taking advantage of a particular offer. It is important to understand that these sales strategies are designed to persuade you to make an impulsive purchase. When it comes to items like shopping, entertainment and dining out, you should be mindful of how much money you are spending. It is best to have a weekly budget that outlines how much you will have left to spend on activities such as shopping and entertainment after saving and paying your recurring household expenses. It is also great to establish how much money is needed for gas, groceries and other miscellaneous expenses. Having all of your obligations outlined will help you gain a better understanding of how much money you can afford to spend on extras like eating out and entertainment. If you are spending a large amount of money on these items and activities, it is time to begin scaling back.

Many people believe that they deserve to splurge, because they work hard. Unfortunately, this mentality can easily cause you to overspend. Working hard does not always equate to earning a salary large enough to splurge on unnecessary items. Furthermore, working hard does not give you free reign to throw your hard earned money away. Frequently investing in things that depreciate in value is a major mistake. If you lose your job or need to take a medical leave of absence, all of the fancy clothing, accessories and electronics will not help you pay your bills. However, you would be able to successfully navigate such financial emergencies if you would have deposited the money spent on unnecessary items into a savings account. I understand that everyone is not in a position to save a large amount of money every month. However, if you take a close look at your spending habits, I am certain that you will find areas of spending that can be scaled back or completely eliminated. After completing a thorough budget analysis, you will likely be surprised to find how much your spending splurges, both large and small, add up to at the end of the month. For example, think about how much you spend dining out. Do you take your lunch to work or do you purchase lunch every day? Another great example is cable. Although many of us think of cable as a necessity, it is actually a form of entertainment. Perhaps you can scale back on the current package that you have or switch to basic cable. I highly recommend that you print out one month of activity for your checking account and examine how much you spend on shopping, dining out, entertainment and so forth. The first time I examined one month of activity for my checking account, I could not believe how much money I wasted. I am not suggesting that you never dine out, shop or spend money on entertainment. However, such purchases should be done in moderation. Furthermore, we should think of creative ways to have fun without spending a significant amount of money.

Saving should be a significant component of your financial management process. If you are not saving for an emergency fund or your retirement, you really cannot afford to dine out, shop or splurge on entertainment. As a woman, I must also acknowledge the fact that we have a category of spending that I refer to as personal maintenance. Personal maintenance includes trips to spas, beauty salons, nail shops and so forth. Although personal maintenance often feels like a necessity, it is actually a luxury. Many women spend money on clothing, accessories, hairstyles and manicures while living paycheck to paycheck. Likewise, there are people living in homes and driving vehicles they cannot afford. If you cannot afford gas or maintenance for a luxury vehicle, please do not purchase it. It is not wise to spend more money than you can afford simply because you would like to impress others. Instead, it is much wiser to have a six to eight month emergency fund. On the other hand, if you can afford to live a luxurious lifestyle and still have a modest savings and retirement account, then by all means continue to do so. But if you are not in a position where you have adequate savings and retirement funding, it is time to take a step back and prioritize your spending. We never know what circumstances or situations will arise. As a result, it is important to strive to accumulate a six to eight month emergency fund that would cover all of your expenses if you were unable to earn an income due to unforeseen circumstances. For instance, if your expenses add up to $2,500 per month, your emergency fund should be between $15,000 and $20,000.

Credit and Debt

In addition to monitoring the amount of money that you spend and creating a six to eight month emergency fund, you should pay close attention to your credit score. It is also important to monitor the amount of debt you have accumulated. Your credit score gives lenders, vendors and employers an idea of how credible you are as a person. As you strive to build a good credit rating, there are a number of principles that you should follow. For example, you should always pay your bills on time. If you pay your bills late, it will be reported to the three primary credit bureaus (Equifax, TransUnion and Experian). It is also important to limit the number of inquires on your credit report. Having multiple inquiries on your credit report, negatively impacts your credit score. Therefore, when a store offers 10 to 15 percent off of your current purchase price for applying for their store credit card, it is wise to politely decline. The offer may sound enticing but every time you take advantage of one of these offers, your credit is pulled and your credit score is impacted. Now, if you are shopping for a car or a home and you are shopping for the best interest rates available within a short time frame, your credit score is not lowered each time your credit is pulled. Therefore, vehicle and home loan shopping is the exception to this rule. Pre-approved credit offers are also an exception to this rule.

Similarly, it is also important to understand that you should never use your credit to purchase a large ticket item, open an account or co-sign a loan for someone else. The issue with engaging in such practices is that you are making a huge financial decision that can have a negative impact on your credit and financial well-being in the future. When we make a decision to purchase a large ticket item, open an account or cosign a loan, it is often based on our relationship with that individual and our belief that the individual will make the required payments. However, what we do not consider is what will happen if the payments are not made. Because it is a loved one, you most likely will just have a verbal agreement, which will not stand up in court. Moreover, how many of us are really willing to take a loved one to court? Furthermore, you must keep in mind that when you co-sign a loan, you are equally responsible for the loan. Therefore, if the other party dies, becomes unemployed, or decides not to pay, you will be responsible for the loan. If the loan is not paid, your credit rating will be impacted and in some cases your wages may be garnished.

As I mentioned earlier, relationships with friends or relatives will be impacted if he or she does not pay the account or loan as agreed. Yes, there is a chance that everything will be paid off as promised. However, this is not a financial risk that you should be willing to take, unless you are capable and willing to pay for the account or loan, if needed. You should also consider not adding family or friends to your credit or bank accounts. Adding someone to your credit or bank account authorizes them to make any purchase they would like to make. Although you would like to believe that a close friend or relative will not be irresponsible with your credit card or bank account, having access to someone else's money can be tempting to someone who is struggling financially. I have made a few mistakes of this nature in the past and had to suffer the consequences. So, keep in mind that the recommendations that I am making are for your benefit. I am a giver and I have made many financial decisions based on emotions and relationships. Unfortunately, when it comes to money matters, we have to make decisions based on our future. Therefore, if there is a possibility that your credit or financial future can be negatively impacted, you should go a different route.

Finally, you should pull your credit report from the three major credit bureau's at least one per year. In the past, I have used www.annualcreditreport.com. This website allows you to review your credit report from all three credit bureaus on an annual basis. Furthermore, you should be aware of your credit score. If you do not know your current credit score, www.creditkarma.com is an awesome resource. Creditkarma.com allows you to view your credit report and credit score free of charge, provides a breakdown of the areas that comprise your credit score, reveals the amount of debt you have accumulated and gives you an opportunity to truly understand why you have a particular score. It also offers budgeting tools that will allow you to monitor your spending and set financial goals. I cannot overemphasize the importance of monitoring your credit and the amount of debt that you have accumulated. If you have a low credit score, you should immediately begin working towards improving your credit rating. I know that many categorize mortgages and student loans as good debt. However, I personally believe that no debt is best. Do I have student loan and mortgage debt? Yes I do. However at this very moment I am diligently working toward a debt free lifestyle.

Changing Your Perspective

This chapter aims to change your perspective on money matters if you have not been financially cautious or budget savvy over the years. However, even if you have been managing your money appropriately, you should continually enhance the skills that you already have related to money management. It is imperative that we begin to be honest about our financial well-being. As with most areas of your life, you can appear to have it all together while suffering in silence. Yes you can mask your sadness, the way you feel about yourself, and even your financial well-being. However, at the end of the day, you know the truth. If you are living beyond your means, you must change your perspective about money and spending. If you have been pampering yourself to the extent that you do not have money to cover an unexpected expense, it is time to change your perspective on money. Once you are honest with yourself, you can begin to repair your finances.

As an individual who enjoys giving and helping others, I must also discuss the act of giving. Whenever I give someone a gift, compliment or just a few encouraging words, it is truly genuine. I do not give expecting anything in return because I find helping others very rewarding. However, if you are also a giver, you must make sure that you are not giving more than you can afford to give. The same rules that apply to spending apply to giving as well. For example, if you are not financially stable, you cannot afford to spend excessively on birthday, holiday and anniversary gifts. To elaborate, if you do not have an emergency fund yet have credit card debt and are barely making ends meet, can you really afford to loan others money? You must be honest with yourself and your loved ones if you cannot afford to loan money. Honestly, it is difficult to say no to a loved one. Particularly, if they are in a situation where they can be evicted, lose their transportation or have their utilities disconnected. In these types of situations, if you can afford to help out, you should. However, you should never put your financial well-being in jeopardy to help someone else. Furthermore, you should not have to rescue the same person more than once or twice. Sometimes we believe that we are helping our loved ones but we are actually enabling them to continue to poorly manage their finances. Perhaps you can encourage that individual to learn a trade, get a part-time job or connect them with a community resource.

The $10,000 worth of credit card debt that I discussed earlier was partially the result of giving money that I could not afford to give. I was renting cars, obtaining cash advances and purchasing items that relatives needed. It was not until I moved to Georgia and attempted to rent an apartment that I understood how much I had ruined my credit. I remember going into a furniture store and being denied for a $1,000 furniture loan. Although, I was eventually approved to rent all of my furniture, I ended up paying more than what the furniture was worth. Even after working in the field of social work for two years, I was unable to obtain a car loan. I was told that I had good income but I was considered high risk and received several denial letters. After going to a local car dealership, I was connected to a local lender who charged me a 24 percent interest rate on a car loan. I was in a situation where I knew that I could not get a loan from anywhere else. I also desperately wanted to get out of my 2000 Kia Sephia, so I agreed to the terms of the loan. It is great to help family and friends when you can afford to do so. However, you must first be financially stable. Financial stability entails having a six to eight month emergency fund, having an ability to pay your credit card debt in full at the end of every month and having the ability to make a monthly contribution to a retirement fund. I truly hope that this chapter helps you gain a better understanding of money management. As you strive to be the woman that God has created you to be, remember to be honest with yourself. Finally, remember that you are capable of being financially stable although it will take discipline, hard work and determination. Once you begin seeing your savings account grow and your amount of debt reduced, you will begin to feel better about your financial future. Your financial health is important and it deserves consistent attention.

My next steps to get to the next level

_____

_____

_____

_____

_____

_____

_____

_____

_____

_____

_____

_____

_____

Child
Sexual Abuse

Many women who are survivors of child

sexual abuse attempt to suppress

or alleviate their pain by intentionally

avoiding the topic. For this reason,

many child sexual abuse survivors

are suffering in silence.

Similar to many of the other issues discussed in this book, child sexual abuse is not discussed enough. There are far too many children and adults in the U.S. and beyond, who are currently suffering from the effects of child sexual abuse. In fact, as many as 25 percent of women in the U.S. have experienced some form of child sexual abuse (Pereda, Guilera, Forns, & Gomez-Benito, 2009). This means that there are millions of women in the U.S. who have had their childhood innocence stolen. It also means that there are a lot of women suffering in silence. The sad reality is that we all know at least one woman who has been a victim of child sexual abuse even if it is not acknowledged. In fact, we probably know several women who are survivors of child sexual abuse. This statistic reiterates and confirms the importance of having an open and honest dialogue on this issue.

Child sexual abuse occurs when a sexual act between a child and an adult takes place and consent is not or cannot be given (Zastrow & Kirst-Ashman, 2010). The sexual act may be by force, deception or the child might actually seem to understand the nature of the activity (Zastrow & Kirst-Ashman, 2010). Finally, a sexual act between two children where there is a significant disparity in age, development or size, is also considered child sexual abuse, particularly when the younger child is not capable of providing informed consent (Zastrow & Kirst-Ashman, 2010).

Many women who are survivors of child sexual abuse attempt to suppress or alleviate their pain by intentionally avoiding the topic. For this reason, many child sexual abuse survivors are suffering in silence. I am now able to identify myself as a survivor of child sexual abuse. However, it was a secret that I managed to keep hidden for a very long time. In fact, my husband was not aware that I was a victim of child sexual abuse until after we were married. Likewise, my experience was not even revealed to my sister, whom I am very close to and love very much. In retrospect, I realize that there was a great deal of shame and embarrassment associated with this particular childhood experience. Based on my personal journey towards sharing all of this, I do understand that child sexual abuse is an issue that can be very difficult to acknowledge and discuss openly.

Despite the difficulty associated with having an open discussion about child sexual abuse, it is imperative that this issue remains at the forefront of our minds. The effects of child sexual abuse often continue well into adulthood. In fact, many survivors struggle to maintain healthy relationships. Difficulty establishing trust, promiscuity and various addictions can also be the result of suppressing the experience of childhood sexual abuse. The aforementioned struggles are simply reminders that the root of the symptom has not been acknowledged and addressed. As women, we must become more comfortable acknowledging when we are in pain. It is important to understand that hidden pain cannot be alleviated. As long as pain remains hidden, it is difficult for it to be totally eradicated.

Children are a vulnerable population and they totally depend on adults to ensure their safety. We cannot ignore the fact that there are sick adults who take advantage of children and steal their innocence. As a social worker, I have encountered numerous children and adults who have been sexually abused. I have also encountered numerous mothers who have been in denial about the fact that, the man they love and share an intimate relationship with, is a child predator. It is often difficult for these women to accept that their boyfriend or even their husband took advantage of their child. I have never been in a circumstance where I was forced to choose whether to believe my child who says that he or she has been sexually abused, or my significant other who denies those allegations. However, as a mother and an individual who knows what it feels like to experience child sexual abuse, I know that the choice would be an easy one.

When we critically examine child sexual abuse, it is important that we avoid the blame game. In most situations, the truth of the matter is one person is an adult and the other person is a child. An adult should never take advantage of a minor and it does not matter if the child is 14 or 15 and believes that he or she is capable of consenting to have sex. In most states, 16 is the age of consent. Therefore, the men and women who decide to have sex with children, even if consent is given, should be charged and taken into custody. Yes, I know that there are times when young girls are dishonest about their age because I was dishonest too. In fact, sometimes I would add a year or two to my age but I was still underage. Unfortunately, many child predators know that their victims are underage and they make it a point to frequent places where young girls or boys will be found. Sadly, they might even become involved in a relationship with a woman who has children, simply for that purpose. If you are an adult, you can easily tell the difference between a 14 year old and an 18 year old. It is very likely that a 14 year old is still in middle school or is just beginning high school. So, this is the first hint that you are dealing with a child. Furthermore, a 14 or 15 year old is likely to be immature and although they are in an adult's body, their thoughts and behaviors are still relative to their age. A teen or a pre-teen has not lived long enough to truly understand the repercussions of having sex. This is why adults need to allow children to be children. It is essential that adults refrain from engaging in intimate relationships with minors, regardless of the minor's willingness to have sex.

My Story

Child sexual abuse is an unfortunate reality. As a result, it took a tremendous amount of courage to put my experience in writing. I have held on to this experience for years, not truly understanding how much harm I was doing to myself. Now I know that my courage and my story might be just what someone else needs to work through a similar situation.

I was an only child for 10 years. My mother was very protective of me and she did not allow me to spend nights with friends. However, there was a well-trusted family member that I loved and enjoyed hanging with. For this reason I was allowed to spend time at her house as often as I liked. Because she had a daughter who was close to my age, we were almost like sisters. She also had a son and he was like my older brother. We spent a great deal of time together and I would spend the night with them often. I was about eight years old when the sexual abuse began. My mom told me to let her know if any man made me feel uncomfortable by touching me anywhere on my body, including my "pocket book," which was her term for vagina. She told me if I informed her about it, she would believe me, even if it was my step dad. I understood and I agreed but the problem was, my perpetrator was not a man. He was my older cousin. I loved my cousin so his actions confused me. However, it was not until I was an adult that I realized that I had been sexually abused.

I was sexually abused quite often by my cousin who was several years older than me. During the day I would play with my cousins and we would have a great time. In the evening, we would watch television, play games, go to church and many other things. However, in the middle of the night when everyone else was sleep, my older male cousin would come wherever I was sleeping and have sex with me. This continued for three years. As I became older, I decided that having fun with my female cousin was not worth what happened once everyone fell asleep. So, I started spending more time with my friends and less time with my cousin. Strangely, during my ninth grade year, we were living with my grandmother and my female cousin and I were attending the same high school. Her brother had dropped out of school at that point but he was still at home. Because my grandmother lived a good distance from my school, it made sense for me to stay at my cousin's house. The plan was for me to spend some nights with my cousin so that I can save my mom some time and gas. However, this arrangement only lasted one night.

I remembered what I had experienced several years back but at this point, I was 14 years old and in the ninth grade. I guess I was just naïve but I really did not think that my older male cousin would still attempt to have sex with me at this point in my life. However, he decided that he would come into the room where I was sleeping in the middle of the night and touch me like he had done in previous years. When I felt him touching me, I woke up. I was caught off guard. I knew that I could not let it continue, so I sat straight up and said "stop right now or I am going to tell my mama." Surprisingly, he got up and left the room. I was proud of myself but I wondered what this might do to our family. The next day I told my mom about what happened. However, I did not tell her about the previous years until I became an adult. She was upset and disappointed that I waited so long to tell her. Looking back, I realize that I followed her instructions literally. She asked that I tell her if a man made me feel uncomfortable. Well, my cousin was not a man but at the same time he was old enough to know that he could take advantage of me. Once I became an adult and came to terms with what happened, I was able to link my experience of child sexual abuse with many of the poor decisions that I made as a young adult. I was also able to connect my experience of child sexual abuse with the various feelings, emotions and behaviors that I never quite understood. If you were sexually abused as a child, this is an issue that you must address. Although you may not believe that being sexually abused has impacted you, it has. Once you come to terms with the abuse, you can grieve, release your anger and discuss your feelings. It is imperative that you do whatever it takes to heal and ultimately forgive. I will go more in depth about the power of forgiveness in chapter six.

Taking Action

The experience that I shared is one that I have suppressed for many years. Though suppressing this experience seemed to help on the surface, it really did not help at all. In actuality, it caused my experience of child sexual abuse to manifest itself in other areas of my life. Women who have experienced child sexual abuse are more likely to have low self-esteem, psychological distress and increased chances of choosing a physically, verbally and or sexually abusive partner (Lamoureux, Palmieri, Jackson, & Hobfoll, 2011). For years, I was not aware that childhood experiences were linked to poor decisions and adverse behaviors during adulthood. For example, I remember telling my husband how some of the pain I currently experience relates to my childhood relationship with my biological father. I talked about how he was always there for my younger siblings who grew up in his household. I talked about how privileged they were to have an opportunity to grow up in an upper middle class family. Yet I, on the other hand, grew up in poverty. Next, my husband's response to these feelings surprised me. While he showed compassion about what happened, he felt that it was something that happened when I was a child and I that I should be over it. At that moment, I shut down and thought, "maybe he is right." Maybe I should be over this at this point in my life. Well, if I had addressed that particular issue, I probably would have been able to move forward. However, just like many of my other issues, I pretended that it did not exist and continued to make everyone, including my biological father, believe that I had it all together.

Equally important, children who are sexually abused might exhibit odd behavior, psychological distress, sexual aggression and anger (Zastrow & Kirst-Ashman, 2010). As adults, we often characterize these children as bad, attempting to be grown or just plain weird. However, these children are crying out for help whether they know it or not. If you continue to look at behaviors on the surface, you might not find out what is going on with a child until it is too late. Over the years, I have worked with a large number of pregnant teens and most of them shared several of the following characteristics: lived in a single parent home, low socioeconomic status, little or no contact with their biological father, premature sexual activity, experienced child sexual abuse, involved in a intimate relationship with an older man. For clarification purposes, I would like to note that having these characteristics does not mean that a child will become a teen parent. However, having these characteristics does place a child at higher risk of becoming a teen parent. Moreover, these are not characteristics that I merely read about these are characteristics that I witnessed while working with pregnant and or sexually active teen-aged girls.

In spite of this being a painful topic for many women to discuss, it is time to stop pretending that child sexual abuse is an act that rarely takes place and begin to take action. We cannot allow this cycle of pain and suppression to continue through generations. Moreover, if you have a child or a child relative, it is very important that you do all you can to prevent them from remaining or becoming a victim of child sexual abuse. The first step you can take to combat child sexual abuse is educate the child on the issue. Children need to be educated about their body and taught to use the correct terms, such as breasts, vagina and penis to avoid confusion. Children also need to be told that they must tell their parents, guardians or another trusted adult if someone has touched or talked to them in a way that made them feel uncomfortable. Parents may feel uncomfortable talking to their children about sex. As a result they may choose to wait and allow schools to educate their children in this area. However, waiting for the school to talk with a child about their body parts or sex is the wrong decision. Unfortunately, if you wait too long, someone may take advantage of the fact that the child is naïve about sex or does not feel comfortable talking about sex with their parents.

The second step involves urging children to tell you or a trusted adult about inappropriate sexual behavior immediately. A trusted adult can be a teacher, aunt, grandmother, etc. Children should understand that they should tell even if the perpetrator has threatened to harm them or someone they love if they tell. Children also need to know that you are there for them and that you will believe them if they ever came to you about sexual abuse. Even if the person making them uncomfortable is your husband or significant other. The final step involves paying close attention to your child or any child that you have established a relationship with. If you notice odd behaviors, isolation, anxiety and so forth, it is time to have a conversation. Whatever you do, do not automatically attribute these behaviors to puberty or hormonal changes. Try to have the type of relationship where the child feels comfortable talking with you because if the child believes that you will respond with anger or extreme shock, they probably will not tell you. Remember to tell the child that it is not his or her fault. The child might believe that it was something that he or she did, that caused the sexual abuse to happen. Finally, if a child confides in you, it does not matter who the perpetrator might be, you must get the police involved. Inform the child that you believe what they have told you. Also let the child know who you will be contacting and why. Although we often talk with our children about strangers, we do not prepare our children enough for the fact that most cases of child sexual abuse involve a family member or a close family friend.

If you have experienced childhood sexual abuse, it is important that you come to terms with your experience and begin the healing process. Like me, you may have suppressed it or do not consciously think about it on a regular basis. However, that does not mean that you have resolved the issues that accompany child sexual abuse. Therefore, it is very likely that you have had some adverse behaviors, experienced emotional distress or have simply made several decisions in your adult life that were a direct result of your childhood experience. If you believe counseling would help you overcome the negative effects of your experience, please contact an experienced counselor or psychologist. Sometimes there is a negative connotation attached to receiving counseling or therapy. However, depending on the extent of the trauma experienced, counseling may be necessary. Next, receiving counseling does not mean that you are a weak person or that you are "crazy." It simply means that you have the courage to engage in an honest dialogue about your situation. It also means that you have the inner strength needed to begin working towards healing and removing the barriers that may be preventing you from enjoying the life that God intended for you.

Finally, be sure to reach back and support someone else who has experienced child sexual abuse. Perhaps you can serve as a mentor or just provide a listening ear. I once heard someone say "it does not cost a candle anything to light another candle." As I stated in the previous chapter, helping someone else can be very therapeutic. Please do not shut down or run away from the topic of child sexual abuse. By confronting this issue head on, we can prevent others from having to experience the pain and silent suffering that we may have experienced over the years. We can also restore broken relationships and help others heal from the emotional distress they endured as a result of child sexual abuse. Holding in anger and resentment can be a huge barrier to happiness, physical and mental well-being. For this reason, it is critical that we begin to take action. I truly hope that you will take action because there are innocent children and hurting men and women who are depending on you.

My next steps to get to the next level

_____

_____

_____

_____

_____

_____

_____

_____

_____

_____

_____

_____

Dating and Intimate Partner Violence

Dating can be an exciting and enjoyable experience for many women. During this period a woman dates one or multiple guys in an effort to determine who would make an appropriate life partner.

Dating can be an exciting and enjoyable experience for many women. During this period a woman dates one or multiple guys in an effort to determine who would make an appropriate life partner. For some women, the dating process is short and sweet. However, for others the dating process can be cumbersome. A good example of a woman who actually had an ideal dating experience is my sister who is 10 years younger than I am. She actually began dating an awesome guy during her first year of college. Now, many years later, they are still together. My sister is an example of a woman who did not have to experience what I experienced in the dating world and that is great. I am extremely proud of her and her accomplishments. Although many women will have the opposite experience, they can begin to make the changes needed to avoid attracting the wrong men into their lives.

I began dating my husband at that age of 27. I do understand that someone 27 years of age is relatively young. However, if you have been dating the wrong type of men for countless years, the dating process can become tiresome and frustrating. Particularly, when physical attraction is the main attribute used to identify a life partner. I constantly made the mistake of choosing men who were physically attractive but did not have much to offer beyond their physical appearance. For example, they often lacked attributes such as honesty, commitment, maturity and faith in God. Honestly, I did have an opportunity to date men who had the qualities I should have been looking for. In fact, I know that if given an opportunity, they would have treated me like a queen. However, if they did not pass the physical attraction test, I would quickly cut ties with them. Now I realize that there is so more to consider when selecting a mate than physical attraction. It is imperative that you examine qualities such as faith, work ethic, honesty and intellectual capacity. After maturing and dating for a while, most women recognize that a man needs to bring more to a relationship than good looks. If a man does not have anything to offer but good looks he is certainly not your best option.

I began seriously dating at the age of 17. I entered college at 17 years of age and became involved with a young man who was extremely jealous and abusive. I believe that my step-father did an awesome job of being a dad. However, he did not always exhibit the positive qualities that a young lady should look for in a husband. For example, he would consume large amounts of alcohol, frequent nightclubs and bars and start arguments with my mom upon returning home. I loved and still love my dad dearly but I would always say that I did not want a man with the same attributes. Instead, I wanted a man who was honest, faithful and not argumentative. Nonetheless, I often found myself dating men with the exact qualities that I despised. As a young lady, I did not truly know my self-worth and I often settled for so much less than I deserved.

During the dating process, it is extremely important not to become so desperate for a relationship that you become willing accept whatever comes your way. It can become frustrating when you have made several attempts to find Mr. Right and he turns out to be Mr. Wrong over and over again. However, this is not the time to begin ignoring red flags. There are times when you have Mr. Wrong and do not see any red flags. However, this is extremely rare. The truth of the matter is that many women choose to ignore red flags. When a woman becomes tired or frustrated with the dating process, she might begin to think that she will never find the right mate and make a decision to settle. Red flags might also be ignored when a woman is eager to get married and have children like I was. There is absolutely nothing wrong with looking forward to marrying and starting a family. I believe that this is a normal desire that many women have. I understand what it feels like to be constantly asked when you will get married and have children. The people who continue to ask you about marriage and children probably married young and cannot understand why you are still single. Times have changed and although it is difficult, smile and reply, "Whenever God blesses me with a husband and children you will be the first to know." I also understand what it feels like to continually witness your peers get married and have children. I have attended weddings and baby showers during times when I felt as though I would never have a family of my own. Despite all of the pressure that we feel to get married, it becomes a serious issue when your desire for a husband begins to interfere with your decision to leave a relationship that is not in your best interest.

Unfortunately, when we seem desperate or eager for someone to love us, the man that we are dating can easily detect that desperation. I have had male family members tell me that they look for women with low self-esteem. Yes, this is very pathetic.

However, there are men out there who look for vulnerable women. Sometimes you might not even realize that your mate is only sticking around because he knows that he can take advantage of you. In fact, he may know that you are willing to accept anything for the sake of being involved in an intimate relationship. Once a manipulative man determines that you do not value yourself and that you are willing to tolerate unacceptable behavior, he internalizes the notion that he can continue to take advantage of you. The moment a man recognizes that you will settle for poor or mediocre treatment, he might cheat, become overly critical or even physically and or verbally abuse you. As a woman you must recognize your value and understand that you deserve to be treated with love and respect at all times. Please do not fall prey to settling for mediocrity.

Though the aforementioned dating advice may seem harsh, I can assure you that I am not oblivious to the fact that men who mistreat women are wrong. Moreover, I am not implying that women are at fault for being mistreated. Instead, I know that there are many men who consistently abuse and mistreat the women in their lives. In fact, there is nothing a woman can do to prevent a serial cheater or aggressor from cheating and or becoming physically aggressive. As women, we cannot change the behavior of an aggressor or a cheater. An aggressor or cheater must be willing to change and seek the assistance needed to change permanently. Next, I want to acknowledge that we should not accept intentional and continual mistreatment. I have repeatedly made this mistake and I would hate for other women to waste time thinking that they can change a cheater, abuser or manipulator. I truly want to convey that settling is not an option. As women, we must know what we will and will not accept from our partners. We must also pay attention to the red flags that are often ignored when we are in the "honeymoon" phase of dating.

My Story

Because I completed high school one year earlier than my original graduation date, I was able to enter college at the age of 17. Unfortunately, I had no idea that I was truly not ready to leave home and live on a college campus. Shortly after arriving on campus, I began dating an extremely popular athlete who was a few years older than I was. The freshmen were on campus for orientation a few weeks before the upperclassmen returned. However, the football players had practice, so they were allowed to return to campus earlier. As a naïve freshmen, we were bombarded by football players but unaware that they already had girlfriends. As a result, I simply melted when I was approached by the guy who would ultimately turn my world upside down.

When the upperclassmen returned, I kept trying to figure out why one particular girl kept looking at me in a confrontational manner. Finally, I was told that it was my current boyfriend's ex-girlfriend. I later found out that she only became his ex-girlfriend after he met me over the summer. After only dating him for a few months, I began to see serious red flags but I ignored them. He became very possessive and wanted to know where I was every minute of the day. My friends would often joke about the fact that I was dating a stalker. Little did we know, his behavior was going to shift from moderate to severe stalking. He literally climbed trees outside of my dorm to make sure that I was in my room. I am not sure how he was able to do it but a few times he just popped up to my room and it was a girls-only dorm. He also managed to figure out how to check my telephone messages from a remote location. I was young and struggling with self-esteem issues, so I thought that he was just trying to show me how much he loved me.

He continued to stalk me the entire time that we were dating. However, he also began to physically abuse me as well. The first time he became physical with me was when I came outside in a very revealing outfit. Of course, he was already standing in front of my dorm. He grabbed me, put his hands around my neck, pushed me and told me that I needed to go back and change. Once I changed my outfit and came back outside, he was fine. He walked me to most of my classes and I would sometimes see him peek through the window on the door. One of my male science teachers actually went outside and told him to stay away from our classroom door. In addition to physically abusing me, he was notorious for fighting on and off campus frequently. For this reason, guys around campus were afraid to talk to me. It was to the extent that guys were afraid to participate in group assignments with me because they were afraid that he would beat them up.

I can think of numerous occasions where he choked and punched me until I fell to the ground. Sometimes it was because I did not answer my phone. Other times it was because I went to a party with friends or because he saw me looking at or talking to another guy. I will never forget a concert experience that started out great and ended horribly. I told him that I was attending a particular concert with my friends and he said that he did not have a problem with it. Once the concert was over, we noticed that several popular rap groups who had performed earlier were on the bottom level of the auditorium. As young college girls, we thought that it would be fun to lean over the balcony and flirt with them. We were all leaning over the balcony, when one of the rappers asked for my number. Of course, I was flattered and I could not resist. However, as I was giving him my number, I felt a blow to my head and it was my boyfriend. I should not have been surprised but I really did not think that he would purchase a concert ticket just to stalk me. One of my friends tried to help me and he hit her too. He was escorted out of the venue and both of us declined to press charges.

Whenever I threatened to break up with him, he would beg me to stay with him. If I told him that our relationship was really over, he would call my friends and ask them to talk to me. He would promise to never do it again and oftentimes buy me a gift or ask to take me to dinner. Typically, after a day or two, I would take him back. He would proceed to be the perfect boyfriend for a month or two and then the cycle would start over again. Interestingly, while in college, I had several friends who were also experiencing intimate partner violence. Even in the midst of my own situation, I would often plead with my friends to leave their abuser. Particularly, because they had actual bruises and had to receive medical attention. Because I did not have physical bruises, I often minimized what was actually happening to me. To a certain extent, I believed that he only hit me when I did something wrong, so it was partially my fault.

My self-worth was very low and I just did not have the strength to leave. I would often think that I would never find a guy who loved me as much as he did. He continued to stalk me while I was in graduate school even though I tried to cut ties with him. The one time I attempted to date someone else, he showed up at my house in an effort to prevent me from going on my date. To make matters worse, he pulled out a ring to try to convince me to marry him. One week after this incident, he put sugar in the tank of my car. Once I finished graduate school, I knew that it was time for me to move on. I began applying for jobs out of state and I was offered a Hospice Social Worker position in Georgia. I really did not want to leave my family but I knew that I had to move to another state in order to officially end all contact with him.

Moving Forward

In order to make wise decisions about who we decide to enter a relationship with, we must take a step back and analyze how we see ourselves. Believe it or not, the way that you view yourself is closely related to how much pain and suffering you are willing to endure in an intimate relationship. If you do not value yourself or have a true understanding of what you have to offer, you will continue to date someone who is a serial cheater. You might also accept verbal and physical abuse. Furthermore, if you do not value yourself or understand what you have to offer, you might be willing to date a man who is already involved in a committed relationship. How you see yourself as an individual impacts whether or not you demand respect or accept being repeatedly mistreated. Perhaps you secretly believe that you cannot do any better than the guy that you are currently dating. Perhaps you believe that you might as well settle for what you have because, "after all there not any good men out there anyway."

Although, I have felt this way before, this is simply not true. My problem was that I would almost always meet guys at a party or a nightclub. As a woman you should try expanding your horizons. For example, go to the gym, go to a museum, go to bookstores, perhaps you can try a new hobby. Sometimes as women we will think of 100 reasons why we should remain in an unhealthy relationship. Yes, it can be difficult when children are involved. However, think about the type of environment that you are providing for your children. I believe that fear is one of the main reasons women stay involved in unhealthy relationships. Fear can prevent you from making healthy decisions and moving forward with the life that you deserve. If money is an issue, begin thinking about how you can use your current talents and skills to increase your income. Perhaps you should consider going back to school. If you are not sure about how to move forward, begin by identifying why you are remaining in an unhealthy relationship. Once you accept the fact that you are in an unhealthy relationship, you can begin to build the strength necessary to move forward.

In the United States, 1 in 4 women have been victims of intimate partner violence and 1 in 6 women have been stalked during their lifetime. These statistics are astonishing and far too high. Again, it is time to break the silence. There are too many women hurting and feeling as though they do not have anyone to turn to for support. If you have never been involved in a physically or verbally abusive relationship, you might find it difficult to understand why the woman being abused will not leave the abuser. Although the decision to leave might be easy for some women, those who have been in an unhealthy relationship for a long time often find it difficult to leave their abuser. If you know someone who is in an abusive relationship, please be patient with them. It is important that you understand that women who are victims of intimate partner violence, often need a great deal of support. There are shelters, counseling, and other community resources available to victims of intimate partner violence. However, in order for any intervention to be successful the victim must truly be ready to permanently end the relationship and move forward. I know from personal experience that the abuser can be very manipulative and can make the victim feel as though the physical or verbal abuse will never happen again. However, if the abuser does not receive long-term counseling, it is very unlikely that the cycle of abuse will end.

I know that this issue impacts teens and adolescents as well. As you read earlier in this chapter, I was only 17 when I first experienced intimate partner violence. Boys who have witnessed domestic violence are likely to be aggressive when they begin dating. My college boyfriend actually witnessed domestic violence often as a child. Subsequently, he ended up becoming physically abusive himself. We must make sure that we talk with adolescents and teens about intimate partner violence. As I mentioned in chapter 1, I began having a negative view of myself during my pre-teen years. Therefore, I was a fairly easy target for intimate partner violence. We must ensure that our girls understand that the media does not define beauty. We must ensure that our girls understand that it is never okay for anyone to physically or verbally abuse them.

Unfortunately, most of the time teens listen to their friends, who are also teens. This is typically not helpful, because most of the time their friends do not have a clue about what is and what is not acceptable. Therefore, when you discuss physical and verbal abuse with a teen or a pre-teen, you must provide a clear definition. Defining physical abuse is important, because being slapped, punched, pushed or shoved a few times might not be considered physical abuse in the mind of a teen. Particularly, when there is not a bruise or when the teen has friends who are experiencing the same thing. Defining verbal abuse is also important, because the music that teens frequently listen to often degrades women. It has become the norm to be spoken to in a degrading manner and our girls do not see anything wrong with being called names that are considered derogatory. In fact, many of the terms that the older generations perceived as negative are actually viewed as normal or acceptable by younger generations. This has lead to a generation of young women who are unknowingly being mistreated

Educating and talking with our youth about their value and self worth is a great way to introduce the topic of intimate partner violence. Considering the prevalence of intimate partner violence it is very likely that you know someone who is currently a victim of intimate partner violence. This is an issue that should never be taken lightly. Many women have lost their lives as a result of intimate partner violence. Unfortunately, many women are embarrassed about what they experience in private, so they decide to suffer in silence. I would like to see women begin to form a true sisterhood. Do not pass judgment on someone who is in an abusive relationship. Do not say, "I can no longer support you if you do not leave right now." Sometimes, you have to just be in a supportive role and slowly empower that person to realize that they do have the strength needed to move forward. From personal experience, I understand that it is not easy to leave, but I also understand that it is important to love yourself more than you love your abuser. Putting distance between me and my abuser was the best decision that I could have ever made. When the relationship that I had with my long-term abusive boyfriend ended, I still loved him. However, I knew that he would never change and I decided to move on. The fact that I left, shows that you can love someone, and still leave.

Was leaving difficult? Yes. Although I was in a different state, I still had a habit of always looking over my shoulder. Although it took a while, I was eventually able to have a life where I did not have to live in constant fear. When you are involved in an abusive relationship, you are always on guard, because you never know when the abuser will decide to strike again. Most importantly, you cannot truly be yourself. Transitioning to the unknown can be scary and uncomfortable, but the reward will be well worth it. Stop for a moment and think about what it would feel like to truly be happy. Now, begin brainstorming the steps that you can take to get to that place.

My next steps to get to the next level

_____

_____

_____

_____

_____

_____

_____

_____

_____

_____

_____

_____

Depression

Depression is a medical condition that interrupts the lives of many men and women. It is another major contributor to the silent suffering epidemic and it is an issue that deserves attention.

Depression is a medical condition that interrupts the lives of many men and women. It is another major contributor to the silent suffering epidemic and it is an issue that deserves attention. Depression has a way of taking the joy out of your daily experiences and can transform a typically happy and outgoing person into someone who is sad and withdrawn. It is important to note that in the United States about one out of every ten adults has been affected by depression. Similar to some of the other issues discussed in this book, depression is not discussed enough. In fact, in many instances mental health is not discussed at all. One reason the topic of depression is often avoided stems from the negative stigma attached to it. However, when you examine the high rates of depression, it is clear that this condition needs to be discussed on a regular basis. Although anyone can be impacted by depression, women are more likely to be diagnosed with depression than men. There are a variety of factors that place women at higher risk for depression. Those factors can be biological, hormonal, environmental, social and so forth. For this reason, researchers are unable to pinpoint one particular reason. However, it has been established that women are more likely than men to have prolonged feelings of stress as a result of negative situations or events. It is also quite common for women to experience anxiety as a result of being emotionally connected to problems experienced by family members and close friends. The hormonal shifts that women experience due to premenstrual syndrome, pregnancy, and menopause also contribute to their increased risk of developing depression.

Being strong is an admirable trait for women to possess but it can be a shortcoming at times. As women, we must try our best to ensure that our physical and emotional well-being remains intact. If we are the bond that holds everything together, what happens if we break down physically or emotionally? We must accept that we are not going to be perfect in every area of our lives. I refer to this relentless pursuit of perfection as the "superwoman syndrome." And, yes, I have been guilty of this too. For instance, there was a time when I was working both a full-time and a part-time job while attending school full time, trying to take care of the cooking, cleaning and grocery shopping among other things. Although, I was able to give myself credit for being a "superwoman," I was overwhelmed and I was tired. But for some reason, I was afraid to admit that I was tired. Fortunately, I now understand that I only stress myself out when I try to accomplish too much at once. In fact, at this point in my life, I ask for help when I need it. My husband enjoys cooking, so now he does most of the cooking. In fact, if he offers to clean the house or pick up our daughter, I will gladly let him do it. I would love to take care of everything but I understand that I cannot and that is my truth.

Depression is not diagnosed when a person is occasionally sad because sadness is an emotion that impacts everyone at some point in their lives. On the other hand, when feeling sad, empty, and hopeless becomes persistent and begins to interfere with your daily activities, this is likely a sign of depression. Signs and symptoms of depression include, but are not limited to the following:

• Persistent sad, anxious or "empty" feelings

• Feelings of hopelessness and/or pessimism

• Irritability, restlessness, anxiety

• Feelings of guilt, worthlessness

and/or helplessness

• Loss of interest in activities or hobbies once

pleasurable, including sex

• Fatigue and decreased energy

• Difficulty concentrating, remembering details

and making decisions

• Insomnia, waking up during the night,

excessive sleeping

• Overeating or appetite loss

• Thoughts of suicide and/or suicide attempts

• Persistent aches or pains, headaches, cramps
or digestive problems that do not ease even
with treatment

Unfortunately, the signs and symptoms described above are oftentimes ignored or written off as stress. As a result, there are millions of women of varying ages and ethnicities suffering from depression in silence. Unfortunately, I know what it feels like to suffer from depression in silence and it is an awful feeling. Depression should be taken seriously, as it can and will impact your physical and emotional health. In fact, if depression is ignored or left untreated, it has the potential to become debilitating. It is extremely important to seek help when you have symptoms of major depression. Major depression might interfere with your ability to work, because it can slow down production and cause you to be frequently absent from work. Major depression also impacts your ability to eat, sleep and enjoy activities that were once enjoyed. Moreover, major depression can lead to loss of relationships, poor health, job loss and even suicide. Dysthymia is a less severe form of depression. However, the symptoms persist longer. For example, individuals with dysthymia might not be in a situation where their symptoms are debilitating but their symptoms might last for two years or longer and prevent them from functioning normally and enjoying their lives.

My Story

Beginning in my early twenties, I began to notice some of the symptoms of mild depression. I have always struggled with frequent anxiety, fatigue and low energy. I have also struggled with feelings of hopelessness. Whenever I experienced a minor setback, I would be hard on myself and I would become extremely discouraged. For some reason, it was quite difficult for me to perceive that I could get through difficult situations. One of the issues that placed me under a significant amount of stress was related to pregnancy loss and infertility. I had always dreamed of becoming a mother, so when I did become pregnant, I was shocked and elated. However, that pregnancy ended in miscarriage and I was devastated. All of the joy and excitement that I experienced quickly faded and I became very depressed. Several years later, I became pregnant again and that pregnancy ended in miscarriage as well. From that moment forward, I envied every pregnant woman in my path. It did not matter if she was a stranger or someone I knew personally. When I had to attend baby showers, the worst part was going to the baby section to purchase a gift. I could not understand how something so cruel could happen to me. In addition to being surrounded by pregnant women, I worked with pregnant teens and teen mothers on a daily basis. Again, I wondered why I was placed in that position when I desperately wanted to become a mother myself. Although I was depressed, I hid it very well. Just like I was able to mask my self-esteem and financial issues, I was able to mask my depression. Over the next four years, I cried myself to sleep almost every night. I would cry in the car, the shower and even in my office. Strangely enough, my mother was probably the only person who had a clue that I was unhappy.

My mother knew that I was struggling because I would talk to her about how badly I wanted to become a mother. I would obsess about becoming pregnant and sometimes I would talk to my mother about it and just break down and cry. I purchased ovulation prediction tests, took my basal body temperature and even visited a fertility clinic. I tried Clomid, which is a fertility drug, and that did not work either. I was in a situation where I could not enjoy life because I was too focused on my fertility issues. Finally, my mother told me that she knew that

I would have a child. However, she told me that I would first need to stop envying other pregnant women and genuinely be happy for them. Initially, her words did not make any sense to me. However, I tried what she suggested. I thought about the fact that some of the women that I saw could have previously experienced infertility issues or suffered from a pregnancy loss as well. I must admit that this was not easy and it took a while for me to truly be happy when someone revealed that they were pregnant. However, although I eventually reached a point where I did not envy women who were pregnant, I continued to exhibit symptoms of depression.

After being married for about nine months, I decided that I was going to pay for an intrauterine insemination (IUI). I was at the point where I was miserable and willing to deplete my savings if it would help me reach motherhood. Well, I believe that God was laughing because he had a plan of his own. I had gone through all of the testing procedures and in June 2011, I was scheduled to have my first IUI. Ironically, my June appointment ended up being a prenatal appointment. I was finally pregnant but I was not as happy as I could have been. I was actually very scared that I would suffer another miscarriage. My doctor was very diligent about giving me progesterone pills and he eventually moved to administering progesterone injections. My entire pregnancy was consumed with fear. I would mark my calendar every day and I did not enjoy my pregnancy the way that I should have. I was extremely grateful and I had a mini celebration at the end of every week. However, it was not until I reached 35 weeks that I felt as though I was really going to be a mother. Again, on the outside, I appeared to have it all together, but on the inside, I was struggling.

Pregnancy loss and infertility were very difficult and painful experiences for me. In previous years, I often wondered what it was like to become pregnant after only a few months of trying to conceive. I also wondered what it would be like to be someone who had never experienced pregnancy loss. However, at this moment there is no doubt in my mind that God has a plan for each and every one of us. Because of my experiences, I realize that it is truly a miracle and a blessing to experience pregnancy and motherhood. There will always be a special place in my heart for the babies that are not here with me today. However, I now understand that God has His own plans and His plans are not always aligned with ours. Although I believe that prolonged sadness is unhealthy, I must acknowledge that there is nothing wrong with grieving the loss of a pregnancy or feeling sad if you are having fertility issues. Nonetheless, there are many men and women who have not had this experience and may not completely understand the emotions that accompany pregnancy loss and infertility. For this reason, family members and/or friends might unknowingly make hurtful comments in an attempt to make you feel better. For example, comments like, "at least you know you can get pregnant" are not comforting at all.

Equally important, my final episode of depression actually caught me off guard. Because I had spent so much time wanting to be pregnant, I never expected to suffer from postpartum depression after giving birth to my daughter. I was very emotional and short-tempered and it did not take much for me to cry or become upset. I suffered with symptoms of postpartum depression for almost one year. This was a very difficult time for me because I had a beautiful baby and I was trying to figure out how I could be depressed when I had finally received the baby that I had dreamed about for such a long time. Once I made it through postpartum depression, I decided that it was time to take control of the life that I have been given. I promised myself that I would put in the work necessary to have a rewarding and joy-filled life. I also came to the realization that I had wasted far too many years of my life suffering from depression. Now, I realize the importance of enjoying the journey of life. We will not be problem-free but we must understand that unhappiness will not resolve our issues. In actuality, unhappiness is a distraction. If unhappiness will not resolve your problem, doesn't it make more sense to at least attempt to enjoy life? It is possible to smile and enjoy your life, even when you are in the midst of a challenging situation. Afterall, we only get one shot at life and we should not waste the time that we have been given. Furthermore, we should stop magnifying our losses and our weaknesses. I challenge you to focus your time and energy on developing solutions and working towards your personal and professional goals. I also challenge you to appreciate and utilize the talents, skills and positive attributes that you possess.

The Power of Forgiving

There is significant power in the act of forgiving. You might wonder how the act of forgiving can be beneficial or even remotely related to overcoming depression. You might even think that the act of forgiving is irrelevant or insignificant to someone who is battling depression. This notion could not be further from the truth. In fact, when you hold, pain, anger, hurt and unforgiveness in your heart, it is impossible to enjoy your life. However, when you decide that you will forgive yourself or someone else for causing pain or making a bad decision, you are actually doing yourself a favor. If you have unforgiveness in your heart, you are hurting yourself more than you are hurting anyone else. In fact, you may believe that you or the perpetrator deserves to be punished and opt to hold on to the past. Remember that it takes a great deal of energy to hold a grudge. Furthermore, when you hang on to a negative situation, you are keeping it at the forefront of your mind and preventing yourself from moving forward. It is important to note that none of us are perfect and we have all made bad decisions. Furthermore, if you have lived long enough, you have most likely done things that you regret. For example, you may have caused someone else a significant amount of pain and heartache. However, if you truly want to enjoy your life, you must forgive and move forward. When you are hurt or disappointed, you should acknowledge what happened, grieve and move forward. Throughout my life I have been constantly informed of the importance of forgiving others, but I never truly understood why. Although we frequently hear how important it is to forgive others, keep in mind that it is also important to forgive yourself. Yes it is important to hold yourself accountable but you cannot let your story end just because you made a bad decision. Yes the people who have hurt you in the past were wrong, but you cannot live your life in the past. Every day brings a new opportunity to live your best life possible. For this reason, you must forgive and move forward

When you fail to forgive, you carry around an invisible weight. This invisible weight can keep you stuck in the past and is actually a major distraction. Refusing to forgive yourself or someone else could prevent you from having true happiness or engaging in functional relationships. The act of forgiveness is powerful because it gives you an opportunity to let go of a negative experience and move past the anger, resentment and bitterness that often accompanies unforgiveness. When you forgive, it does not mean that you agree with what has taken place. It also does not mean that you must restore the relationship that you once had with the individual who hurt you. Forgiving simply means that you no longer hold a grudge and that you are ready to move forward. Once you truly forgive, you will feel better. I can say this with confidence because I experienced a situation that I did not believe I could overcome. In fact, I kept telling myself, there is no way that you could forgive this person after all of the pain that you have had to endure. I was angry, I was quick tempered, I could not focus at work and I could not stop crying. However, after about one week of replaying the event over and over in my mind, I knew that I had to move forward. I set aside some time to be alone and I made the decision to forgive, even in the midst of my pain. I knew that I could not hold on to the anger any longer because it was literally stealing my joy. I refused to waste another day feeling sorry for myself. I have endured many disappointments and heartaches. However, I have always come to a place where I was forced to forgive and move forward or remain stuck in the past. Forgiving is not an easy task but it can be done. If you make the decision to forgive, you will be on your way to truly enjoying your life.

Moving Forward

There are four key strategies involved with moving beyond depression. First and foremost, you must acknowledge your struggle. Second, you must seek help and support. Third, you must begin practicing positive emotional and physical health habits. Fourth, you must make a commitment to pursue happiness and understand that moving beyond depression takes time. If you or a loved one is currently experiencing signs or symptoms of depression, remember that these symptoms should not be ignored. Furthermore, feeling depressed does not mean that you are odd or inferior to anyone. In fact, accepting that you are struggling with symptoms of depression shows tremendous strength. If you have a friend or family member who exhibits symptoms of depression, please be as supportive as you possibly can. People respond and cope with depression in various ways. For example, someone who is depressed might cope by drinking alcohol, overeating, becoming withdrawn, abusing prescription drugs and/or abusing illegal drugs. Unfortunately, the aforementioned coping mechanisms only mask the symptoms of depression. When you utilize poor coping mechanisms, you never really address the source of your depression. Suppressing and/or ignoring the symptoms of depression often prevent both men and women from moving forward. Acknowledging that you struggle with depression can be a difficult step. However, without acknowledging that you have symptoms of depression, the process of healing cannot begin.

It is important to seek help and support when you experience symptoms of depression. You can overcome the symptoms of depression if you take action. Perhaps you feel most comfortable talking with a close friend or family member. If this is the case, remember that the most important step that you can take is to seek help and support. Fortunately, there are various resources available to assist with the symptoms of depression. However, counseling and medication are the most common methods of treating depression. Support groups are also an option. Joining a support group will connect you with others who are experiencing similar issues. If you are not sure where to start, you might want to contact agencies or organizations who can provide services or link you to the services that you need. In fact, there are organizations that will provide counseling services regardless of your ability to pay. Your local hospital, department of children and family services, or health department can often link you to counseling resources within your community. If you would prefer to be counseled through your church, that is also an option. Additionally, it might also be helpful to contact your primary physician, as he or she may be able to refer you to counseling resources within your community as well.

Practicing positive emotional and physical health habits promotes longevity and are beneficial to everyone. Practicing positive emotional habits involves being grateful for what you do have, not depending on others to make you happy and seeking to maintain a positive attitude, even when you have negative or hurtful experiences. I can think of many times when a perceived negative experience led to something better than what I initially lost. Many times we cannot see past our current situation and we allow ourselves to get hung up on our disappointment. Maintaining a positive attitude and keeping an open mind will allow you to be in the frame of mind necessary to move beyond the past and into the future. If you maintain a negative attitude or continue to focus on your disappointments, you will be too distracted to identify a solution to your issue or concern.

Next, exercise can help relieve anxiety because it releases natural, "feel-good" endorphins. The endorphins released during exercise boosts your mood, helps you relax and can help you sleep better. Perhaps you can take a fitness class or find an exercise buddy. Socializing with others might also take your mind off of your problems and help improve your mood as well. Finally, exercising gives you an opportunity to release any anger or hostility that you might be holding in. When I am feeling down, I often just want to be alone and there is not anything wrong with wanting to be alone for a short period of time. However, if you are spending a significant amount of time alone, you should at least attempt to interact with a friend or loved one. Equally important, being inactive and not being cautious about what we put into our bodies actually increases our stress levels. Also keep in mind that poor health habits increase the risk of being diagnosed with illnesses such as hypertension, diabetes and heart disease. Unfortunately, having health issues will only add to the amount of stress that you already have. As women we can become extremely busy and feel as though we do not have enough time to eat healthy or exercise. The solution is to set realistic and attainable goals. For instance, you increase your chance of failure by setting unrealistic goals such as: transitioning from an extremely sedentary lifestyle to exercising for one-hour everyday or deciding to completely eliminate all of the foods that you enjoy from your diet. Although it is possible to reach such goals, such an approach will lead to frustration and increase the chances of you quitting your new regimen.

Instead, it is best to set S.M.A.R.T. goals. S.M.A.R.T. goals are specific, measurable, attainable, reasonable and time sensitive. I have found that keeping healthy snacks around, substituting sugary drinks with water and cutting back on bread and/or fried foods is a great nutritional compromise. I have also found that exercising 20 to 30 minutes three to four days per week is sufficient. There are days when I cannot exercise a full 20-30 minutes. When this is the case, I exercise 10-15 minutes in the morning and 10-15 minutes in the evening. Exercising 3-4 days per week gives me the physical activity that I need to reduce my stress levels and remain healthy. Increasing your physical activity, even if it is not rigorous, will be beneficial to your overall health.

The final strategy involves making a commitment to happiness and understanding that moving beyond depression takes time. It is easy to teach and recommend this principle. However, it takes a significant amount of effort to abide by this principle. Overcoming depression and committing to happiness is challenging, but it is not impossible. There are days when I am hit with issue after issue and really have to work hard to keep a positive attitude. However, there are other days when everything goes well and it's easy to maintain a positive attitude. When you make a commitment to happiness, you must keep in mind that no matter the circumstance, you will keep pushing forward. Change is not easy and setbacks happen. However, a setback does not mean failure. It is during those difficult times when you must fight for your happiness. Moving beyond depression is not an overnight process. Therefore, you should give yourself time to heal and implement some of the strategies discussed in this chapter. In the beginning, it might seem as though you have more bad days than good days. However, if you continue to fight for your happiness, your good days will begin to greatly outweigh your bad days.

My next steps to get to the next level

_____

_____

_____

_____

_____

_____

_____

_____

_____

_____

_____

Education:
A Powerful Force

Education is indeed a powerful force. During the current economic times, education is extremely important. Our educational background often determines whether or not we will have a career or job. Our educational background also impacts our access to financial and social resources.

Education is indeed a powerful force. During troubling or uncertain economic times, education is extremely important. Our educational background is often the determining factor in whether or not we will have a flourishing career. Our educational background also impacts our access to financial and social resources. Past and present research findings have made it clear that earning a high school diploma is essential. Educational researchers have also found that dropping out of high school is a decision that can negatively impact a person's future experiences. During the 1960s and 1970s, having a high school diploma was considered a valued asset in the labor force (Kaufman & Chapman, 2004). However, in recent years, having a high school diploma has become a minimum requirement for entry into the labor market (Kaufman & Chapman, 2004).

Having this knowledge, we must consistently reaffirm the importance of continuing to educate ourselves beyond high school or GED programs. Therefore, if you have not pursued postsecondary opportunities, it is time to begin thinking about the next phase of your career. I understand that college may not be for everyone. However, it is paramount that you find a skill or passion that can be utilized to expand your options and marketability after completing high school. For example, you can enroll in a community college, university, the military or a trade school. It is important to make the transition quickly. In fact, when you have goals and a desire to enhance your career . opportunities, you should never procrastinate. Procrastination should be avoided, because it can prevent you from taking action and ultimately pursuing the postsecondary opportunities that are available.

In addition to pursuing postsecondary opportunities, it is important to read often. Reading is critical to expanding your knowledge base. It is also a great resource that enhances your knowledge about the various issues that have a direct impact on the lives of some of our most vulnerable populations. Reading can engage you and take you places that you might not ever physically be able to visit. It also promotes open-mindedness and provides you with a better understanding of the perspectives and beliefs of others. Finally, reading expands your vocabulary and enhances your critical thinking skills. Education is an extremely important asset for women because it expands our thoughts and ideas, which gives us a broader understanding of our capabilities. Education also expands our career options and our overall marketability. As a woman, you should make continuing education a lifestyle choice. We should never believe that we are too old to learn or try something new. Even in this era, women are still fighting to be viewed and treated as equal to men in the workplace and beyond. Additionally, women are more likely to be the primary or only caregiver for their children. Without adequate education and training, there is a strong likelihood that you will be forced to settle for a low-paying job. Having a low-paying job can be frustrating and can lead to physical and emotional health problems. For this reason, it is extremely important that women take advantage of additional training, skills and certifications. Women must be in a position to make enough money to provide for themselves and their families. At this juncture, you can begin to see how inadequate education and training can cause women to suffer in silence.

I am a strong proponent of education in terms of earning a high school diploma, certification in a particular skill or college degree. However, I also believe that education goes far beyond striving to earn a degree or certification. In fact, one of the greatest benefits that education brings is the awareness that you still have more to learn. When we examine some of the issues in society such as sexual harassment in the workplace, poverty, intimate partner violence and HIV/AIDS, we find that women are impacted at disproportionately higher rates than men. The fact that women are at a higher risk for these issues reveals that women have risk factors that men are not susceptible to. For example, a woman who is in an abusive relationship and totally dependent on her partner financially is in a high risk category for being infected with HIV. To elaborate, a woman in this situation may be aware of her partner's promiscuity but she is not in a situation where she can refuse sex or negotiate safe sex. 20 years ago the most at-risk group for the HIV and AIDS virus were homosexual men. However, today, heterosexual women are the most at-risk group for the HIV and AIDS virus. In fact, the Center for Disease Control (CDC) (2010) found that women account for 20 percent of new HIV infections in the United States. For this reason, women must continue to educate themselves on a regular basis. In essence, education equips women with the knowledge and tools needed to protect their physical, emotional and financial health.

How Education Changed My Future

It is an honor to be able to share how education changed my future. I am proud to say that I never lost sight of my love for learning, even when I encountered tremendous losses and struggles. While in high school, college, graduate school and even in my doctoral program, I encountered struggles that could have prevented me from graduating. However, I remained focused in spite of the barriers that came my way. It is important to understand that we cannot allow the distractions and struggles of life to prevent us from reaching our goals. I did not always make great decisions. In fact I was notorious for making bad decisions. However, I remained determined to pursue my educational and career goals. I knew what it was like to struggle financially and I wanted a lifestyle where I did not have to worry about meeting my financial obligations and needs. As I reflect on the impact that education has had on my life, I realize that it has allowed me to break the cycle of generational poverty. Education has also allowed me to transition from being dependent upon others for financial support, to actually having a career with unlimited potential. It is clear that I would not be where I am today without education.

I always knew that I wanted to attend college, so during my senior year of high school I filled out and submitted an application to Benedict College. I initially majored in education. However, after learning about the field of social work from a friend, I changed my major to social work. I did a significant amount of partying but I still managed to graduate with honors. Our teachers constantly pushed us to apply for and enroll in a graduate program because most employers preferred the Master of Social Work degree (MSW). One of my most memorable professors, Dr. Nicholas Cooper-Lewter, recommended that I apply for the Advanced

Standing MSW program at Barry University in Miami and I did. I was even able to earn a partial academic scholarship during my tenure at Barry University. Upon entering the advanced standing program, I had a great deal of family and financial struggles. I tried working part-time but found it to be extremely overwhelming since the program was very intense. The advanced standing MSW program is intense because it is a two year program that is condensed into only one year. While pursuing my MSW, in addition to struggling financially, I lost an aunt who was like a second mother to me and my dad (step-father) was diagnosed with kidney failure. However, I persevered and graduated on time with a 3.75 GPA. My academic performance at Barry University helped dispel a comment made by one of my undergraduate professors during my internship. I always strived to earn A's, which my internship field supervisor awarded me with. However, my professor awarded me a "B," when I inquired about the "B," she told me that I was a "B" student. Well, from that point forward, I was on a journey to prove her wrong and that is exactly what I did.

After completing graduate school, I began searching for jobs. I applied for jobs in Florida, Georgia, South Carolina and California. Surprisingly, I received calls and job offers from multiple agencies. I knew that I needed to move out of South Florida and I knew that I did not want to live in a major city. Therefore, when I was offered a hospice social worker position in Georgia, I was beyond excited. At this point in my life, I was beginning to reap the benefits of my hard work. I was able to find a nice apartment and thankfully the apartment complex was running a special that offered a free first month of rent. Additionally, due to the special offer, the apartment complex did not require a security deposit. Unfortunately, my poor credit rating did not allow me to take advantage of that offer. After being told that I would need to pay a security deposit, I had to call and ask my biological father to help me financially. Although I was always willing to help others, I absolutely hated asking for help. My father agreed to help me and I was able to pay my security deposit and purchase a few household items. I did not have anything, so my mom gave me a few of her household items and made sure that I at least had a mattress. Since I was not accustomed to living a middle class lifestyle at that time, my living situation did not seem dire. Instead, I was happy and content because I knew that I would eventually be able to purchase the items I needed.

Working as a hospice social worker allowed me to earn a good salary, begin contributing to a savings account and support my family financially. Working as a hospice social worker also allowed me to begin repairing my credit. After working with hospice for about a year and a half, I became interested in working with children and families. When a school social work position was advertised in the newspaper, I applied for it. However, I really did not believe that I would be called back. Several months after submitting my application, I was called back and a few weeks after interviewing, I was offered the position. God works in mysterious ways because I was competing against highly experienced social workers for the position. On the other hand, I had very little experience in the field. However, I was selected and my new position offered a higher salary, while working only 10 months per year. Once I actually began working in my position, I realized how much I enjoyed working in the field of education. After a few years of working as a school social worker, I was able to pay off most of my consumer debt and qualify for a home loan. The only debt that I carried was a car loan and a student loan.

For years I considered pursuing a doctoral degree but I was not sure if it was something that I could actually accomplish. Interestingly, my paternal aunt enrolled in a doctoral program and told me that I should at least call to find out more about the program. I took her advice and called and went on to submit an application. I was accepted into the program and subsequently enrolled but it took me a while to complete the program because there were several terms where I did not take any courses due to various circumstances. In fact, I actually took a six month break after entering my second trimester of pregnancy. Pursuing a doctoral degree is not an easy task. It requires a tremendous amount of time, dedication and financial resources. Nevertheless, the benefits of earning a doctoral degree far outweighed the temporary sacrifices I had to endure. Pursuing a doctoral degree allowed me to begin working as an adjunct professor. It also allowed me to earn two pay raises. Pursuing a Ph.D. was very intense and the dissertation process was stressful at times. I even had to pay for my last three terms out of pocket. However, it was all worth it when I had the opportunity to finally reach my goal, walk across the stage and celebrate my accomplishment. Despite all of my struggles and setbacks, I graduated with a 4.0 GPA. I often think back to the times when I felt like I would never make it through the dissertation process. What if I had given up prematurely? My story is a true testament of what can happen if you refuse to give up. It is also a testament of the power of education.

Pass It On

As a social worker and mentor, I am a strong advocate of helping our youth understand the importance of education. I am also an advocate of connecting youth with positive role models. Even though I was considered an at-risk youth, I had three major protective factors in place. First, I had a mother who was supportive and a strong advocate for education. Secondly, I enjoyed learning and third, I had a strong desire to attend college. Unfortunately, many at-risk youth do not have those protective factors. In fact, many at-risk youth do not have any contact with a positive adult role model. Research related to mentoring at-risk youth suggests that a mentoring relationship can help underachieving or disadvantaged youth realize their potential (Little, Kearney, & Britner, 2010). This is great news. However, most mentoring programs have long waiting lists because there are not enough adult mentors. If you do not believe that you would be interested in volunteering for a formal mentoring program, perhaps you can establish a relationship with a youth that you believe has great potential but needs guidance.

Adolescents and teens might believe that they are invincible. Yet, as adults, we know that their futures are at stake. We know that they are negatively impacted by social media, bullying, dropping out of school and engaging in sex at an early age. Of course youth are often under the impression that they know everything. We also understand that they are under the assumption that most adults, including their parents do not have a clue about living in today's society and life in general. However, we cannot sit back and allow them to destroy their futures. Even if they seem to be unappreciative of what we have to offer, we cannot give up on our youth. As an adult, it is important to encourage youth to remain in school and understand the importance of education. Our girls are essentially at-risk of becoming victims of some of the very topics discussed throughout this book. As a result, we cannot take the topic of education lightly. Experience is a great teacher. However, by educating our youth, we can decrease the likelihood of them experiencing the pain, disappointment and heartache that accompanies issues such as intimate partner violence and poverty among other things. Moreover, as women, we have a duty to pass on our wisdom. Educating, encouraging and offering a listening ear can make a major difference in the lives of our youth. Will you answer the call?

As we grow older and mature, we realize that we had a skewed view of life as teens. We also realize that some of the advice that we dismissed could have saved us from experiencing a lot of the pain and heartache that we ultimately experienced. Although there is much to be learned in school, school does not adequately prepare youth for the real world. For example, more times than not, students only face suspension for infractions like fighting, stealing and even bringing drugs on campus. However, in the real world, you are likely to go to jail and have a criminal record for the same offenses. Once you have a criminal record, it is difficult to obtain employment and depending on the charges, you could be disqualified from receiving financial aid. When a student is unable to receive financial aid, this greatly diminishes the likelihood of them attending college. This scenario happens far too often. All of these issues are connected to the significance of mentoring. We cannot place the responsibility of preparing our youth for adulthood exclusively on schools. Furthermore, we cannot wholeheartedly rely on schools to help our youth understand the importance of education. Sometimes we cannot even rely on the parents to help our youth understand the importance of education. As a school social worker, it saddens me when I meet parents who do not value education. However, when I see that a child lacks guidance and support, I am willing to step in and do everything within my power to keep that child in school.

There are youth who are engaging in risky behaviors because they are hurting, looking for love and lacking guidance. Today, there are countless girls who believe they are required to send inappropriate pictures and have sex with their boyfriend. They have this belief because no one has taken the time to tell them the truth, which is the fact that they are beautiful and valuable. How can we expect a girl to truly understand her self-worth when she has continually been exposed to music, videos and a culture that consistently degrades women? It takes a mentor to teach an adolescent or teenaged girl that her value and beauty is not defined by what she might see on television, social media or in magazines. As a mentor, you can dispel the idea that wearing revealing clothing is the only way that a girl or woman can receive attention. Educating our youth is a community effort. It is easy to play the "blame game" when it comes to educating and guiding our youth. Yes, parents and schools probably could do more to guide youth in the right direction. However, there are many opportunities for the community to assist with educating our youth. Are you identifying and offering solutions or merely offering criticism and being an onlooker? I challenge you to take action. I challenge you to take the time to guide a youth in the right direction. The future of our youth is far too important for anyone to remain on the sidelines. Saving our youth should be a community effort.

In addition to serving as a mentor, make sure that you also seek a good mentor. Your mentor should not be someone who will not have the time to interact with you on a regular basis. An interaction can be in-person, via video conferencing, by phone or by e-mail. It took me a while to truly understand the importance of having a mentor but now I understand that it is imperative. In fact, I currently have more than one mentor. Having a mentor can provide you with the same benefits that you are providing the younger generation. Your mentor should be an individual who has qualities, characteristics and accomplishments that you would like to have one day. Your mentor should be someone who can provide you with advice, problem solving strategies and objective feedback. For instance, if you would like to be a teacher or author, an ideal mentor would be an established teacher or writer. Furthermore, a mentor can help you remain on track and may be able to help you reach your goal(s) quicker.

When you are mentored by someone who is experienced in your field of interest, you are likely to avoid some of the mistakes or roadblocks that a typical inexperienced individual will encounter. Your mentor might even have connections that can help you obtain an internship or an entry level job within your field of interest. A mentor is essential for any woman who is ready to transition to higher levels personally and professionally. Your mentor can help guide and encourage you when you feel like giving up. Your mentor can also push you to not only reach, but exceed your goals while placing you on a path to continual learning and growing. There is great value in having a mentor and the time you spend seeking and connecting with a mentor will be time well spent.

My next steps to get to the next level

_____

_____

_____

_____

_____

_____

_____

_____

_____

_____

_____

8

Restoration and Transformation

Life is the most precious gift that we have and we should truly live every day with purpose. In preparation for the challenges and opportunities that lie ahead, it is imperative that you begin incorporating a new way of thinking and living right now.

Life is the most precious gift that we have and we should truly live every day with purpose. In preparation for the challenges and opportunities that lie ahead, it is imperative that you begin incorporating a new way of thinking into your daily life. Do not give up on or postpone your dreams. If you have feelings of inadequacy, emptiness, or hopelessness, take the stance that you will no longer allow these feelings to drive your decisions and actions. You are capable of living your best life right now, but you must be willing to keep pressing forward even when life gets tough. In this chapter, we will discuss the benefits of restoration and transformation. Restoration is defined as the act or process of returning something to its original condition, by repairing it. Restoration is also defined as the act of returning something that has been stolen or taken. Perhaps a physical item, a job or a person has been taken from you and you cannot understand why. Sometimes, things happen that are far beyond our comprehension. In these situations, the item, the job, or person might not be returned. However, that does not mean that you cannot return to or exceed your previous level of functioning. The word restoration is extremely powerful, because it does not have any limits. For this reason alone, life is worth living. As long as you are still breathing, you still have an opportunity to make a comeback. It should be exciting to know that your joy, confidence, energy, and zest for life can be restored. If you do not give up, you can take back what has been stolen and become a person that you did not know existed within you. In essence you can transform your dream into your reality! As I reflect upon the woman that I have become, I know without a doubt that restoration and transformation is possible.

We cannot address restoration and transformation without highlighting resilience. Resilience involves having the ability to bounce back after a struggle or a painful experience. When you encounter a struggle or disappointment, you might subconsciously play the victim role, excessively think about the situation or just settle for mediocrity. Working towards resilience and restoration takes work, just like everything else in life. If you have experienced a significant loss or a traumatic event, you will have good days and bad days. Grief is a process and there is not a specific timeframe for grief. However, your periods of grief will gradually decrease in intensity. Although loss is extremely painful, it is imperative that you expect to enjoy life again. Always keep in mind that your expectations shape your reality. When faced with a challenge, always set realistic goals and be sure to celebrate the small victories. We often focus on our lack of progress, but we should really be focusing on how much we have progressed and even more so, how much we have already accomplished. For example, when reviewing your to do list, do you acknowledge what has been accomplished or do you focus on the tasks that you have not been completed yet? When you transform your thinking, you will be more in tune with your approach to problem solving. You will also be more aware of the times when you excessively dwell on the negative. Your mind has probably become accustomed to your previous way of thinking. Therefore, the process of changing your thinking will take time. Even when you have made a permanent mind shift, your mind will sometimes revert back to your old way of thinking. When this happens to me, I take note and revise my thinking. The good news is that you will ultimately become more conscious of negative thoughts and begin to counteract them with positive thoughts.

Overcoming Barriers

Low self-confidence, fear of the unknown and lack of faith are inclinations that significantly contribute to the epidemic of suffering in silence. If you have or are currently susceptible to any of these inclinations, you have identified your greatest barrier. Before you can be restored and transformed you must begin to break down the barriers that are holding you back. Low self-confidence directly impacts every area of your life. Confidence is not an optional attribute. You must believe that you have everything that you need to reach your goals. You must be able to sincerely feel beautiful and not just pretend to be happy with your appearance. If there are some things that you would like to improve about your appearance and they are within your control, work on those areas. However, you must learn to accept those areas that cannot be changed as a unique asset. Begin by increasing your inner confidence. Once your inner confidence is evident and you have embraced your uniqueness, everyone around you will notice. As a confident woman, it is imperative that you step out of your comfort zone and let your true-self shine.

For years, I struggled with low self confidence. In college, my response to low self confidence was wearing provocative clothing. As a college graduate and professional, I responded to low self-confidence by shifting to a monotone wardrobe. I primarily wore dark colors, because they were within my level of comfort. If I needed to run an errand, I might wear jogging pants, my most comfortable shoes (old of course), and a huge t-shirt. I would think, well I am just going to the grocery store, the mall, or to pick up something to eat. I had become the exact opposite of the person that I was in college. In retrospect, I did not realize how important it was that I look presentable when going out. I believe that this is an important component, because transformation should occur on the inside as well as the outside. What if you unexpectedly met someone with a much needed resource or connection at your local grocery store, mall, or restaurant? What might they observe about your appearance and demeanor? You only have one very short opportunity to make a first impression. It is not important that you wear expensive clothing or shoes. The priority is that your appearance relays the confident, new you. For example, you might wear a casual shirt and jeans, instead of jogging pants and an oversized t-shirt. Be sure to leave a positive and lasting impression with everyone that you meet. Connections are critical, as they can assist you with making your vision a reality.

Similar to low self-confidence, fear of the unknown and lack of faith are barriers as well. It is difficult to make progress, when you fear the unknown, because you are primarily focused on what might go wrong. Likewise, it is difficult to make progress when you do not believe that everything will work out in your favor. By taking a negative stance, you significantly increase your stress level and clearly communicate your lack of faith.

Moreover, when you fear the unknown and truly believe that your situation will not work out, you have already decided that you will not have victory. It is unwise to discount your available resources and supports in advance. Having an optimistic view about your outcome significantly reduces your likelihood of giving up. Having an optimistic view also allows you to focus on the positive skills, attributes and resources that you already possess. To illustrate, you might affirm your relationships, spirituality, creativity and so forth. If you are experiencing a lack of faith, meditate on obstacles and challenges that you overcame in the past. What skills, resources, or supports did you utilize to overcome your previous challenges? If you need to rebuild your faith, you should begin by reflecting upon your previous victories and accomplishments. If you have accomplished a goal or overcome a challenge in your past, you already have what you need to overcome any present or future challenge. Your perceived view of your future can be the factor that determines whether you move towards restoration or remain broken and unfulfilled.

The Path to Restoration and Transformation

In an effort to ensure that you live your best possible life, I will share five strategies that will place you on a path to restoration and transformation. Strategy one requires that you have an ascending mindset and strategy two requires that you continue to push forward in the midst of fear. Next, strategy three requires that you focus on your strengths and strategy four requires that you seek social support. Lastly, strategy five requires that you make self-care a priority. If you are ready to be restored and transformed, you must go beyond reading the strategies that I provide. In order for these strategies to be beneficial, they must be implemented.

The first strategy entails acquiring an ascending mindset. An individual who has an ascending mindset is always searching for a way to learn, grow and excel. An ascending mindset is flexible and is not easily discouraged. An individual with an ascending mindset believes that anything is possible. When you have an ascending mindset, you realize that failure is not an indication that your goal cannot be reached. In fact, when you have an ascending mindset, you view failure as an opportunity to grow and obtain the wisdom needed to revise your strategy. The opposite of an ascending mindset is a rigid mindset. Someone with a rigid mindset has a limited view of what can be accomplished. Although individuals with an ascending mindset and a rigid mindset might have the same opportunities, their perceived and actual outcomes differ tremendously. A great example of this difference is typically revealed when a disappointment or barrier presents itself. I will use the process of obtaining a doctoral degree as an example, because the doctoral process can be extremely challenging. I know several people who enrolled in a doctoral program, took a few classes and quit. I also know several people who completed all of the required coursework, but became discouraged during the dissertation phase of the program and gave up. The individuals who gave up were just as capable of those who persevered. However, those who gave up lacked the frame of mind needed to endure the rigors of the dissertation process. When your perception of what you can accomplish is limited, you are likely to view setbacks and disappointments as the end of your journey. The dissertation process requires that you be able to accept a large amount of criticism. It also requires that you submit and re-submit your proposal several times, even when you believe that what you initially submitted was your best effort. A rigid mindset would think, "I cannot do this, it is impossible to make it through this process." By comparison, an ascending mindset views the dissertation process as an opportunity to grow. When you have an ascending mindset, you understand that there is a difference between not reaching your goal and not yet reaching a goal. Lastly, when you have an ascending mindset you are willing to embrace the process of goal attainment, knowing that you will eventually reach your goal.

The second strategy entails pushing forward in the midst of fear. When you push forward in the midst of fear, you are pursuing restoration and transformation. Moreover, my pastor, Dr Maurice Watson describes fear as "False Evidence Appearing Real." Fear can cause you to forfeit your growth, restoration, and transformation. In effect, fear prevents you from reaching your full potential. Fear is not an emotion that we can prevent. In fact, everyone experiences fear at some point in their lives. Therefore, our goal must not be to remove fear, but to have the drive needed to push through our fears. In other words, you should never allow fear to hold you back. When I made the decision to write this book, I was excited, but I was very afraid. I was afraid, because I was leaving my comfort zone and entering a new experience. I have written a dissertation, but I have never written a book before. **Moreover, I was quite hesitant about sharing my story. I could have easily succumbed to my fears** but I decided to push through them. In essence, I pushed forward in the midst of fear. When you feel fear and still push forward, you ignite your strength and improve your self-confidence. The first step is always the most difficult step to take. Once you take the first step, your strength will gradually be revealed to you and you will begin to wonder why you waited so long in the first place. Although you might not notice, others are watching you. Your strength can help restore and transform someone else's life as well.

The third strategy entails focusing on your strengths and abilities. Have you ever taken the time to identify and write down your strengths? Do you focus on your strengths and abilities more than you focus on your weaknesses? There are many benefits that accompany identifying and building upon your strengths. However, one of the greatest benefits that result from concentrating on your strengths is achieving restoration and transformation. It would be awesome if we could obsess about our strengths, instead of obsessing about what is wrong with our lives, our bodies, our partners, and so forth. If we would just channel our energy into refining and further developing our strengths, we would be in a great place emotionally. What if you were so focused on being grateful for your strengths that you did not have time to focus on your weaknesses? When you maximize your strengths you automatically boost your level of gratitude, confidence, and life satisfaction. Maximizing your strengths also brings you brings closer to discovering your purpose. When you discover your purpose, you actually have a specific area where you are able to utilize and share your unique talents and skills with others. Becoming engrossed in your strengths allows you to recognize your potential for growth and positive change. The next time that you are tempted to point out a weakness or a perceived deficit, remember that you are more likely to overcome an obstacle when you focus on the strengths that you bring to the situation. I am not suggesting that you become totally oblivious to your weaknesses. I am simply challenging you to become fixated on your strengths, goals, and opportunities. I also challenge you to utilize your time and effort wisely. Do not waste your valuable time and energy complaining about your problems and shortcomings. Be sure to channel the time and energy that you have available into developing solutions and further developing your strengths.

The fourth strategy that will place you on a path to restoration and transformation is social support. Social support can be provided through friends, family, churches and other community organizations. When you seek and maintain social support, you are positioning yourself for a victory. It is imperative that you maintain a support system and ask for help when you need it. It can be tempting to keep your goals and your challenges to yourself. A few reasons people do not seek support is because they do not want to burden others with their issues or because they might feel embarrassed if they fail to meet the goals that they have announced. If you have this type of mindset, it will be difficult for you to pursue your passion. Instead, you must take calculated risks and remain confident that failure is not an option for you. When you make excuses for not sharing your goals or asking for help, you run the risk of remaining in your current situation. Sometimes, the only barrier to your breakthrough is lack of guidance and support. Regardless of how accomplished or financially secure a person is, they will need guidance and support at some point in their lives. If you think about it, even professional athletes, actresses, and singers have coaches. There are times when you need significant support. However, there are also times when you just need a listening ear. Perhaps you simply need a responsible individual to watch your kids for an hour or two while you take a much needed break. Although you might consider yourself invincible to some extent, you must also consider the physical and emotional consequences that accompany doing too much too often. Asking for help when you need it is not a sign of weakness but a sign of strength.

The fifth and final strategy requires that you prioritize self-care. Self-care can be defined as the act of taking care of yourself. Keep in mind that you are your greatest asset. When you are not your best self, everything and everyone around you is impacted. It is well-known that women are naturally inclined to be nurturing towards others. However, it is equally, if not more important that we nurture ourselves. To be more specific, women must make self-care a priority in the midst of taking care of everything and everyone else. There are many components to self-care. However, I will identify what I believe are non-negotiable components of self care: incorporating rest and relaxation, being mindful of your food choices and engaging in regular physical activity.

Rest and relaxation is the self-care component that women seem to neglect most often. There are many days when I am guilty of pushing myself too far. When this happens, I feel a shift in my mood and there is an overwhelming feeling of needing to rest. I have found that giving my body adequate rest is typically what I need, in order to revitalize myself physically and emotionally. I am awake by 5am on an average day and have found that I always feel restored after sleeping between seven and eight hours. However, the optimal amount of sleep needed to varies from person to person. In addition to ensuring that you receive an adequate amount of rest, you should also strive to relax as often as the opportunity arises. Taking a short nap, a walk in the park, or simply sitting in a serene room while reading a magazine or a book, are a few ways that I revitalize my mind and body. Finding convenient and effective ways to relax dispels the notion that a vacation or weekend getaway is needed to achieve this goal. In fact, it is often the small breaks that help us rest and restore our energy throughout the day. At a minimum, you should seek to spend 45 minutes to 1 hour alone at least three times per week. However, I highly recommend finding time alone daily, even if it is only for 10-15 minutes. If you have children, you might need to seek more creative ways to spend time alone. For example, it might just be that your time alone is in the shower, on your lunch break, or during your commute to and from work. Keep in mind that your time alone is not an opportunity to work on a task or make a quick telephone call. This is your opportunity to rejuvenate your mind and enjoy a necessary break. Perhaps you can meditate, listen to relaxing music or listen to a motivational cd. The overall goal is to nurture yourself regularly, spend some time alone and reach a state of relaxation as often as possible. It is an amazing feeling, when you are able to take a few minutes during the day to nurture yourself.

Food choices and physical activity are also critical components of self-care. Are you mindful of your food choices? Do you frequently engage in some form of physical activity? Appropriate nutrition and exercise are non-negotiable components of self-care as well. When you are constantly on the go, it becomes relatively easy to eat food without thinking about its nutritional value. I find that I make better food choices when I am cognizant of everything that I eat. For example, when I enjoy my favorite food, french fries, I am fully aware that I am making an unhealthy selection. For this reason, I am able to limit myself to a small or a medium order of fries. There are also times when I decide that it is in my best interest to eat oven-baked fries, instead of the traditionally cooked french fry. I also keep this selection in mind when making a decision about what to eat for my next meal. However, there was a time when I was not in tune with what I ate and would order large meals without thinking twice. Now, I am more likely to order a smaller portion and drink water instead of drinking the other beverage options. Making small changes in food selection and portion selection can make a major difference in your overall health. Healthy eating should be a lifestyle choice versus something that you only engage in when you would like to lose weight. As we age our lifestyle choices become even more vital, because we are more susceptible to heart disease, hypertension, diabetes, and other illnesses. Aging also means that our metabolism slows down. Therefore, we must eat less and exercise more in order to prevent unwanted weight gain. As much as we like to blame genetics for our health issues, research has consistently revealed that many of the health issues impacting both men and women can be prevented.

The same principals that apply to healthy eating apply to physical activity as well. It is easy to put off physical activity if you are constantly busy and on the go. However, when physical activity is placed on the back burner for too long, it virtually becomes obsolete. This is why it really helps to have an accountability partner. Particularly, if you are one who finds it difficult to consistently make positive lifestyle choices. One way that you can squeeze physical activity into your hectic schedule is by waking up 45 minutes earlier than usual. I know that this will take discipline, but if you develop this habit, you will be more consistent and begin to reap the benefits quicker. If you are one who enjoys staying up late, you might need to go to bed earlier, to ensure that you consistently wake up 45 minutes earlier than usual. Exercising in the morning is your best option if you do not have an accountability partner. Similarly, if you plan to exercise in the evening, you must hold yourself accountable. Especially since evening workouts make you more susceptible to scheduling conflicts and feeling too exhausted to exercise. Whichever option you choose, be sure to hold true to your goal. For individuals who are interested in shedding a few pounds, sparkpeople.com is a great resource. Sparkpeople. com is an online community that helps you monitor and reach your weight loss goals free of charge. In order to optimize your transformation, it is imperative that you remain mindful of your food choices and the amount of physical activity that you engage in on a daily basis. Regular exercise and proper nutrition will enhance your appearance and confidence. However, the health benefits are ultimately the most important benefits of regular exercise and proper nutrition.

A Story of Restoration

I would like to include a heartfelt, powerful, real-life story of restoration in this chapter. Sharon (name changed for confidentiality) is a dear friend and colleague of mine with an amazing and inspiring story. She always maintained the belief that she would overcome her obstacles regardless of how menacing or challenging they seemed. Moreover, her ability to remain strong, joyful and calm during troubling times is extraordinary. Sharon is a breast cancer survivor and I am delighted to share her story as an inspiration to women who are seeking restoration. There will be times when life tosses unfathomable events and situations at us with little to no warning. However, it is during these times

that we activate our faith and decide that we will not give up on life.

I interviewed Sharon over lunch, and our discussion began with the day that she was informed of her breast cancer diagnosis. She revealed that she was so shocked that she could not process her surroundings or what was being explained about her condition at that moment. In fact, she said it actually felt like an "out of body experience." To make matters worse, her diagnosis actually came one week before the one year anniversary of her sister's death. In defiance of these unfortunate events, Sharon came to terms with her diagnosis and according to her, "it was not a why me situation, but more God give me the strength." There was so much uncertainty that she had to make a deliberate decision to maintain a positive attitude. She knew that it was not in her best interest to drown in self pity. For this reason, she chose to believe that everything would be okay. In the midst of dealing with her diagnosis, taking chemotherapy and radiation, the doctors also found a mysterious spot on her lung and a tumor on her brain. All of these devastating events occurred within a period of less than one year. Sharon went from working full time in an administrative position, to missing a great deal of time from work. The first treatment that she received caused her hair to shed and to her surprise, her eyelashes and eyebrows began to shed as well. She went from having long beautiful hair, to not having any hair. However, Sharon vowed not to feel sorry for herself. Instead she went on to take a beautiful picture of herself with a shaved head and embraced her new look. Additionally, Sharon had to undergo four surgeries and she was hospitalized on two occasions.

Although Sharon was weak and undergoing treatment for breast cancer, she continued to work part-time. Everyone was absolutely amazed by her strength and ability to smile, when there was so much uncertainty about the future of her health and even her career. I believe that you will find the strategies that Sharon utilized to cope with her diagnosis very helpful. These strategies are not only for individuals confronted with cancer or other life-threatening medical conditions. These strategies are flexible enough to be applied to any challenge or circumstance. In addition to helping her cope, many of the strategies that she utilized also helped her restore her physical and emotional well-being. As I interviewed Sharon, I noticed that her strategies were significantly aligned with many of the strategies that we have discussed throughout this book. Sharon's strategies included, activating her faith, joining a support group, asking for help when she needed it and allowing herself to have quiet time.

Sharon found joining a support group to be very beneficial. She reported that she was able to interact with women in different phases of their diagnosis. Having a support group allowed her to support others, while also receiving support. Sharon also enjoyed having an opportunity to ask questions and learn more about the risks and side-effects of various medications as well as some of the procedures that were a component of the treatment process. Sharon wanted me to share that even though she was strong, she did have her moments. In her words "even the strongest person breaks down periodically, you must get it out." Again, as I have stated before, holding your feelings inside or pretending that there is not an issue, will not help you move forward. It was during the times when she struggled the most, that she realized how much she needed social support. Sharon was not afraid to ask for help or prayer. In fact, she reported being in constant contact with her pastor, throughout the treatment process. In addition to asking for help, Sharon also activated her faith. Sharon reported that her mentality was "I got this." When you activate your faith, you do not have any doubt that you will have victory over your situation or circumstances. Finally, Sharon believed that allowing quiet time helped her restore her physical and emotional well-being too. She carved out quiet time for herself everyday and she vowed to focus on herself. Just like many of us, she was the person that others called when they had an issue or concern. However, she decided to let go of everyone else's issues, so that she could work on getting back to her previous state of health.

Today, Sharon is working full-time again and has just as much joy and energy as someone who has never endured breast cancer. From the beginning of her struggle, she firmly stated that she did not want any pity. She did not want anyone crying or telling her how sorry they were that she had been diagnosed with breast cancer. In other words, she never accepted the role of victim. In fact, she was a victor from the beginning and she continues to live a victorious life. Even after completing her treatment, she had to have an additional surgery, to remove benign tumors from her feet. Over time, the tumors became bothersome, making it difficult for her to walk. However, she never complained and always kept a smile on her face. I hope that you are as inspired by Sharon's story as I am. Her story affirms the importance of expecting victory in every aspect of your life.

My next steps to get to the next level

_____

_____

_____

_____

_____

_____

_____

_____

_____

_____

_____

_____

_____

9

Conclusion

Conclusion

If I ask you to defend your happiness, what would that mean to you? Does the idea of defending your happiness sound a little extreme? Does it sound like work? I hope that it sounds like work, because, just like everything else in life, it takes work to be happy. Your state of happiness should be deliberate and intentional. There will be moments of difficulty and even disappointment. However, you cannot allow those moments to consume you and hold your happiness hostage. One sure way to defend your happiness, involves distancing yourself from people who are always negative.

Have you ever been in an awesome mood, because something exciting happened? Did you pick up the phone to call a friend or loved one to share your good news? What happens next is very important. Either the person on the receiving end is excited for you or not. Unfortunately, within minutes, your joy and excitement can be sucked right out of you. This has happened to me, many times. Now I recognize the importance of surrounding yourself with positive people. I intentionally limit my time spent around people who are negative and pessimistic. I still love them, but I must do so from a distance.

Perhaps you can begin connecting with like-minded people who always seem happy and full of energy. Take a minute to reflect upon the people whom you spend the most time with. Are they pushing you to grow or are they bringing you down? Connecting with someone who is happy and goal-oriented is a great way to defend your happiness. Today, I challenge you to develop three ways that you can defend your happiness. Once they are developed, place them where you can see them and keep them at the forefront of your mind. Choosing to be happy, will create the positive energy needed to enhance your relationships, your career, and your overall well-being.

Women should not feel the need to pretend to be happy, confident, financially secure, and so forth. Instead of pretending, your goal should be to make your dreams a reality. In order to break free from pretending, it is important that you are honest with yourself and stand in your truth. Are you willing to identify and confront your issues? You must begin working towards living your best life right now. It is not enough to talk about what needs to be done. You must take action. Although we are often tempted to strengthen our weaknesses, we must remember to refine and improve upon our areas of strength as well. Do you know what your strengths are? If so, are you utilizing your strengths to seek out and begin walking in your purpose? We are all placed on this earth for a reason, but many of us never live up to our full potential. Instead of settling for mediocrity, you should be striving to live your best life. Moreover, you should be seeking your purpose and pursuing your passion. We all have gifts, talents, and skills. Are you using the gifts, talents and skills that you have been given? If not, please do not let another day pass without taking action.

I truly hope that this book has exceeded your expectations. As I have stated several times, what I want most is to see you put the principles and strategies that I have shared into action. We have discussed many issues, obstacles and struggles that can weigh you down. We have discussed stressors and major sources of pain. We have also discussed the various ways in which you can move forward when you are in the midst of a challenge. I believe that you are equipped with everything you need in order to become your best self. However, the transformation process should never end. Continue to seek and refine the strengths that are connected to your passion. Pursue your goals and continue to grow. I never want to reach a place where I feel as though I do not have any room to grow. I enjoy learning and although it can be difficult, I often push myself out of my comfort zone. I often think about my move from Florida to Georgia. I did not know anyone in Macon, GA. Now over 10 years later, I realize that moving to Georgia was one of the best decisions that I could have made at such a young age. I stepped out on faith, not knowing what the future held in store for me. Amazingly, I now have just as many connections in Georgia as I do in Florida. God is good. Never allow fear to hold you back. If you take the first step, God will take care of the rest. If I ask you to defend your happiness, what would that mean to you? Does the idea of defending your happiness sound a little extreme? Does it sound like work? I hope that it sounds like work, because, just like everything else in life, it takes work to be happy. Your state of happiness should be deliberate and intentional. There will be moments of difficulty and even disappointment. However, you cannot allow those moments to consume you and hold your happiness hostage. One sure way to defend your happiness, involves distancing yourself from people who are always negative.

REFERENCES

Almeida, C., Johnson, C., & Steinberg, A. (2006). Making good on a promise: What policymakers can do to support the educational persistence of dropouts. *Jobs for the Future*, 1-20.

American Psychological Association (2013). Effects of poverty, hunger, and homelessness on children and youth. Retrieved from http://www.apa.org

Bandura, A. (2000). Self-efficacy. *Harvard Mental Health Letter*, 4, 4-6.

Centers for Disease Control and Prevention (2012). Depression. Retrieved from http://www.cdc.gov

Centers for Disease Control and Prevention (2010). Intimate partner violence. Retrieved from http://www.cdc.gov

Damour, L.V. (2013). Strengths vs stressors. Independent school, 72(4), 82-87.

Henderson, N. (2007). Resiliency in action: Practical ideas for overcoming risks and building strengths in youth, families, and communities. Ojai, CA: Resiliency In Action, Inc.

Lamoureux, B.P., & Palmieri, P.A., & Jackson, A.P., & Hobfoll, S.E. (2012). Child sexual abuse and adulthood-interpersonal outcomes: Examining pathways for intervention. Psychological Trauma: Theory, Research, Practice, and Policy, 4(6), 605-613.

National Institute of Mental Health (n.d). Women and depression: Discovering hope. Retrieved from http://www.nimih.nih.gov

Posovac, S.S., & Posovac, H.D. (2002). Predictors of women's concern with body weight: The roles of perceived self media ideal discrepancies and self-esteem. *Eating Disorders, 10:153–16.*

Ready, D.D. (2010). Socioeconomic disadvantage, school attendance, and early cognitive development: The differential effects of school exposure. *Sociology of Education, 83(4), 271-286.*

Sorensen, M.J. (2006). *Breaking the chain of low self-esteem* (2nd ed). Wolf Publishing Company.

Sullivan, T.P. (2013). Think outside: Advancing risk and protective factor research beyond the intimate-partner-violence box. *Psychology of Violence, 3(2), 121-125.*

Swann, W.B., Chang-Schneider, C., & McClarty, K.L. (2007). Do people's self-views matter? Self-concept and self-esteem in everyday life. American Psychologist, 62(2), 84-94.

U.S. Census Bureau (2013). Poverty. Retrieved from http://www.census.gov

Zastrow, C.H., & Kirst-Ashman, K.K. (2010). Understanding human behavior and the social environment (8th ed). Belmont, CA: Brooks/Cole

COACHING

What is Coaching?

Coaching is a process that helps clients, groups and organizations maximize their full potential. Coaching is not therapy, consulting or mentoring. A coach does not advise or counsel. Coaching is future oriented and results driven. If you are seeking solutions and strategies, coaching is for you!

What are the Benefits?

A coaching relationship is considered a partnership. A major benefit of working with a coach is your ability to become a more productive individual. However, in addition to becoming more productive, you will also gain clarity, increased confidence, and much more. Are you are seeking a breakthrough in any area of your life? If so, coaching can help.

Coaching Programs

Career Clarity
Money Matters
Health and Wellness
Self-Confidence
Self-Discovery

Dr. Houston offers individual and group coaching sessions. If you would like to maximize your potential, contact Jessica Houston Enterprises to schedule a consultation.

Jessica Houston Enterprises

PO Box 2143 Macon, GA 31203
Email: drhouston@expectingvictory.com
Phone: (866) 779-1987

Made in the USA
Columbia, SC
05 November 2024

45612076R00085